PERFECT ENDINGS

Chocolate Dessert and Beverage Cook Book

From the Test Kitchens of
The Nestlé Company, Inc.

©Copyright, 1962
by The Nestlé Company, Inc.

*Designed and produced
by Western Printing and Lithographing Company
All photographs by George Lazarnick*

Library of Congress Catalog Card Number 62-19144

Contents

INTRODUCTION 4

SPECIAL SEMI-SWEET TECHNIQUES 6

One

CAKES, BEAUTIFUL CAKES 8

Any Flavor, As Long As
  It's Chocolate 9
Cakes With a Festive Air 16
Frostings, Fillings and Glazes 21

Two

THE VERY BEST COOKIES 30

Toll House Cookies 31
Extra-Delicious Bar Cookies 41
Real Cool Refrigerator Cookies 52
Happy Holiday Cookies 57
World-Wide Treasury of Cookies 64
Quickies for the Crowd 72

Three

PIE MAKING IS AN ART 88

Prize Chocolate Pies 89
Dreamy Creams and Heavenly Chiffons 93
Gala Party Pies 97

Four

DESSERTS YOU'LL TREASURE 104

Family Favorites 105
Subtle Soufflés, Mousses and Tortes 122
Dessert Pancakes, Waffles, Doughnuts 126
Saucy Sauces and Tempting Toppings 128

Five
CANDY—SWEETS FOR THE SWEET 134
Everyone's Favorite—Fudge 135
Candy Classics 138
Christmas Is for Candy 142

Six
FABULOUS FOODS FROM YOUR FREEZER 148
Frozen Dessert Delights 149
Treats for Tots 162
The New Old-Fashioned
   Ice-Cream Parlor 164

Seven
BEVERAGES—PLAIN AND FANCY 168
Coffee 'Round the World 169
Cocoa—The Universal Flavor 175
Tea—The Cup That Cheers 176
More Hot and Cold Refreshers 181

INDEX 185

Introduction

What fragrance can ever match that of the kitchen of your childhood? The most exotic of spices, the rarest of perfumes, can never produce the pleasure-filled memories called up by the aromas of freshly-baked cake, cookies, candies and brownies.

And, somehow, it's dessert we remember when we think of the meals that marked the festive days in our lives. We remember always the big beautiful birthday cakes that symbolized the happy years of growing up. We remember the fudge we made for our first beau, the cookies out of the pantry after school, the candy shared by brothers and sisters, the hot cocoa at bedtime, the festive engagement cake made by loving hands. How many friendships have been strengthened at afternoon teas, at confidential "coffees," with spur-of-the-moment snacks!

Americans are traditionally hospitable, and nowhere is our hospitality more typically American than in its spontaneous spirit. We no longer feel, as our parents did, that we must entertain on formal occasions only. Ours is the casual "drop-in-any-time" approach of backyard barbecues, for which a quick dessert can be whipped up and served at a moment's notice.

Today, the "hand that rocks the cradle" also runs the family car, brings the local PTA to

order, serves cake at the Community Fund tea, and performs countless other routine tasks. *You*—the American homemaker—also find time, somehow, to cook divinely, to look fresh and charming for your husband and guests. You combine the best of the old and the new by making full use of all the modern appliances and techniques at your command—those time-saving wonders of which your mother never heard. You use the packaged miracles at hand, and to each you add your own touch. Somehow, *your* pudding right out of the package bears only the slightest resemblance to the original product. Enriched by chocolate morsels and a topping of whipped cream, it comes to the table as an appetizing tempter. Your freezer (even in the smallest refrigerator) can hold the makings of delicious, imaginative meals, leaving you time to run your life with ease.

If you are a young homemaker, you start out with the added confidence that the modern test-kitchen has taken the guesswork out of baking and cooking. You know that you can cook creatively, achieving the delicious results your grandmother did—in far less time, and with a minimum of effort. Whether you learn at home or in a classroom, the satisfaction of cooking for those you love is a lifetime source of pleasure which can contribute immeasurably to your sense of fulfillment.

This book is a compilation of treasured recipes—some as old as America, and some as new as tomorrow. We are happy to think that PERFECT ENDINGS will help to provide just that—perfect endings to perfect meals.

Special Semi-Sweet Techniques

There is—as you know—one top flavor. For cake, cookies, candy, ice cream, or pie—chocolate is the one unquestioned winner of the popularity poll. It's appetite-tempting, thoroughly satisfying. Unsweetened, sweet, milk, or semi-sweet, chocolate has no equal—and of them all, semi-sweet rates highest. It's a masterful blend of unsweetened chocolate, sugar, and added cocoa butter. Whether it is used in its morsel form or melted as a frosting, glaze, glamor-decoration, semi-sweet offers you a new era of discovery in the kitchen.

When the Toll House cookie, almost overnight, gained enthusiastic acceptance from American housewives, Nestlé recognized that a new concept of baking had sprung almost full-fledged into being. This concept introduced new American trends, created a huge new industry, and revolutionized cookie, candy, and cake baking. Today millions of attractive, uniform, semi-sweet morsels come to you in the familiar yellow cellophane package. Recipes in this book utilize semi-sweet morsels in many varied ways. We hope that you will find still more uses for them to give added pleasure to every meal you serve in your home.

Are there rules for cooking chocolate?
Indeed there are rules for using semi-sweet chocolate in cooking and most of them are based on the fact that chocolate dislikes high temperature. Chocolate, when cooked at too high a temperature, burns and scorches easily. If heated too fast it may not melt smoothly.

To melt

(a) in large quantity of liquid—follow directions in recipe. (You will need at least ¼ c. of liquid to blend properly with one 6-oz. pkg. of Semi-Sweet Chocolate Morsels.)

(b) with no liquid added, place contents of a package of Semi-Sweet Chocolate Morsels in a double boiler or small bowl. Then set over hot (not boiling) water.

Note:
1. Use dry bowl and rubber spatula or spoon. Guard against rising steam.
2. If semi-sweet should stiffen, add 1 to 2 tbs. vegetable shortening, and stir till smooth.

To store

Chocolate has a rich content of cocoa butter, and therefore should be stored in a cool dry place at a temperature of not over 78°F. If the temperature rises a few degrees above, the cocoa butter will begin to melt and rise to the surface of the chocolate as a shiny coating. As the chocolate cools again, the cocoa butter turns a misty gray color which is known as "bloom." While this does not affect the flavor of chocolate, "bloom" dulls the rich brown, true chocolate color. However, don't hesitate to use chocolate which has "bloomed," for in melting, it regains its attractive color.

Cakes, Beautiful Cakes

"What every woman knows ..." is that even the simplest meal can be made memorable by its dessert. And if that dessert is a big, handsome cake, luscious with frosting, chances are that the meal — or the party — will rate as an unqualified success.

Just *reading* the recipes on these pages will make you eager to get into your kitchen—the sooner to share with your family these delectable cakes. You'll find, among others, dark velvety devil's food, fudge cake of marvelous texture, nut crumbed coffee-cake, an unusually rich Luxury Loaf, and a festive fruit cake. They are all designed to bring you enthusiastic requests for seconds—and for the recipes which produced them.

Here, too, are recipes for the most taste-tempting frostings, glazes, and fillings that ever turned a plain "boughten" cake into the most glamorous of desserts. Chocolate, butterscotch, mocha, fudge, cream, strawberry: swirl any one of these over a square of sponge cake for delicate petits fours, or heap a child's table with colorful cup cakes. These recipes are sure to turn up time and again on your family's most-wanted list.

We have rounded out our chapter with how-to instructions that will simplify for you many tricks of the professional cake-decorator's art, with delightful results.

We hope that you will sample each of these recipes, for we know that many of them will become family heirlooms to hand down to your daughters — and to their daughters.

Any Flavor, As Long As It's Chocolate

DEVIL'S DELIGHT CAKES
Preheat oven to 350°F.

CAKES

MELT over hot (not boiling) water
  1 12 oz. pkg. (2 c.) Nestlé's Semi-Sweet Chocolate Morsels

SIFT together and set aside
  ½ c. sifted flour
  1 tsp. baking powder
  ¼ tsp. salt

BLEND
  6 oz. cream cheese, softened
  1½ tsp. vanilla
  ¼ c. firmly packed brown sugar

BEAT in one at a time
  2 egg yolks

ADD
  Flour mixture
    alternately with
  ¼ c. water

ADD
  Melted semi-sweet

BEAT till stiff but not dry
  2 egg whites

BEAT in gradually till stiff and glossy
  ¼ c. firmly packed brown sugar
Fold into semi-sweet mixture

Line twenty-four 3″ cup cake pans with fluted paper baking cups. Fill approx. ½ full
BAKE at: 350°F.
TIME: 15 to 20 min.

TOPPING

BLEND well
  2 to 3 oz. cream cheese*
  1 tbs. Nescafé
  2 tbs. brown sugar
  Dash salt

BEAT in
  1 egg yolk
  1 tsp. vanilla

BEAT till stiff but not dry
  1 egg white

BEAT in gradually till stiff and glossy
  2 tbs. brown sugar

FOLD into Nescafé mixture
  Egg white mixture
  1 c. heavy cream, whipped
Spread on cakes

YIELD: 2 dozen

*Use one 8-oz. pkg. or three 3-oz. pkgs. cream cheese for Cakes and Topping

(See illustration 23)

page 10 / cakes

DEVIL'S FOOD CAKE

Preheat oven to 375°F.

SIFT together 3 times and set aside
 1¾ c. sifted flour
 1¼ tsp. baking soda
 1 tsp. salt

MELT over hot (not boiling) water
 1½ 6-oz. pkgs. (1½ c.)
  Semi-Sweet Chocolate
  Morsels

Remove from heat

BLEND
 1½ c. firmly packed brown
  sugar
 ⅓ c. soft butter
 1½ tsp. vanilla

ADD, one at a time, beating well
after each addition
 2 eggs

STIR in
 Melted semi-sweet

ADD
 Flour mixture
  alternately with
 ½ c. buttermilk

ADD and stir to blend
 ¾ c. boiling water

Pour in two greased 8″ or 9″
layer cake pans

BAKE at: 375°F.

TIME: 25 to 30 min.
(See illustration 3)

SWISS CHOCOLATE CAKE

Preheat oven to 375°F.

COMBINE and stir over low heat, till
well blended
 1 6-oz. pkg. (1 c.) Semi-Sweet
  Chocolate Morsels
 ¼ c. water

SIFT together and set aside
 2¼ c. sifted flour
 1 tsp. baking soda
 ¾ tsp. salt

COMBINE and beat till creamy
 1¾ c. sugar
 ¾ c. soft butter or margarine
 1 tsp. vanilla

BEAT in, one at a time
 3 eggs

BLEND in
 Semi-sweet mixture

STIR in alternately in small amounts
 Flour mixture
 1 c. buttermilk

Pour into three greased and floured
8″ or 9″ layer cake pans

BAKE at: 375°F.

TIME: 25 to 30 min.

Cool

Frost with Chocolate Cream
Frosting *(see page 22)*
(See illustration 7)

DOUBLE MARBLE CAKE
Preheat oven to 375°F.
COMBINE and stir till smooth; set aside
- ½ c. Nestlé's EverReady Cocoa
- 2 tbs. boiling water

SIFT together and set aside
- 2½ c. sifted cake flour
- 2 tsp. baking powder
- 1 tsp. salt

COMBINE and beat till smooth
- ½ c. soft shortening
- 1½ tsp. vanilla

BEAT in gradually
- 1 c. sugar

BEAT in, one at a time
- 2 eggs

ADD
Flour mixture
  alternately with
1 c. milk
Pour in two waxed paper-lined 9″ layer cake pans

DRIZZLE back and forth over both layers
EverReady mixture
Run spatula or knife through batter to marbleize

BAKE at: 375°F.

TIME: 20 to 25 min.

Cool in pans on wire racks 10 min.
Remove from pans, peel off paper. Cool thoroughly on racks
Fill and frost with Cocoa Cream Frosting *(see page 23)*

CHOCO-DATE CAKE
Preheat oven to 350°F.

COMBINE and set aside
- 1 8-oz. pkg. dates, chopped (1¼ c.)
- 1 c. boiling water
- 1 tsp. baking soda

SIFT together and set aside
- 1¾ c. sifted flour
- ½ tsp. salt

COMBINE and beat till creamy
- 1 c. sugar
- ½ c. soft shortening

ADD and beat till well blended
- 2 eggs
- 1 tbs. grated orange rind
- 1 tsp. vanilla

ADD
Flour mixture
  alternately with
Date mixture

STIR in
- ½ 6-oz. pkg. (½ c.) Semi-Sweet Chocolate Morsels

Turn into well-greased and lightly floured 13″ x 9″ x 2″ pan

SPRINKLE with
- ½ 6-oz. pkg. (½ c.) Semi-Sweet Chocolate Morsels
- ½ c. chopped nuts

BAKE at: 350°F.

TIME: 35 to 45 min.

Serve plain or sprinkle with sifted confectioners' sugar

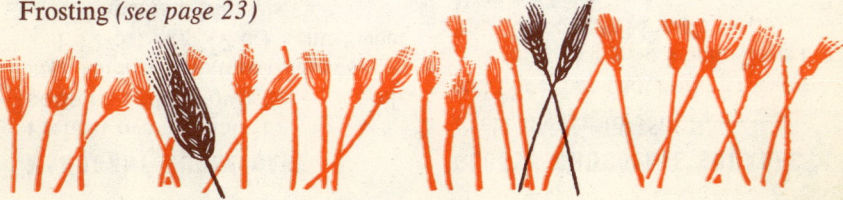

page 12 | _cakes_

MAHOGANY FUDGE CAKE

Preheat oven to 350°F.

COMBINE and stir over hot (not boiling) water till mixture thickens
  1 12-oz. pkg. (2 c.) Semi-Sweet
    Chocolate Morsels
  ½ c. hot water

ADD and cook 2 min., stirring constantly
  2 tbs. sugar
Cool to lukewarm

SIFT together 3 times
  1¾ c. sifted flour
  1 tsp. baking soda
  1 tsp. salt

COMBINE and beat till creamy
  ⅔ c. sugar
  ¼ c. butter or margarine

BEAT in, one at a time
  3 eggs

STIR in
  ½ of flour mixture

ADD
  Remaining flour mixture
    alternately with
  ⅔ c. water

STIR in
  Semi-sweet mixture
  1 tsp. vanilla
  1 tsp. red food coloring
Pour in two greased 8″ or 9″ layer cake pans

BAKE at: 350°F.
TIME: 25 to 30 min.

Cool

Frost with Butterscotch-Cream Cheese Frosting _(see page 24)_

GLOSSY CHOCOLATE SQUARES

Preheat oven to 350°F.

MELT over hot (not boiling) water
  1 6-oz. pkg. (1 c.) Semi-Sweet
    Chocolate Morsels
Remove from heat

SIFT together and set aside
  2 c. sifted flour
  2½ tsp. baking powder
  1 tsp. salt

BLEND
  1 3-oz. pkg. (⅓ c.) cream cheese
  ¼ c. shortening

ADD gradually
  1 c. sugar

BEAT in, one at a time
  2 eggs

STIR in
  Melted semi-sweet
  1 tsp. red food coloring

ADD
  Flour mixture
    alternately with
  1 c. milk
  1 tsp. vanilla
Spread in greased and floured 13″ x 9″ x 2″ pan

BAKE at: 350°F.

TIME: 35 to 40 min.

Cool

Frost top with Chocolate Butter Frosting _(see page 23)_

Let stand till Frosting sets

Cut in 2″ squares

YIELD: 24 squares

CHOCOLATE PECAN CRUMB CAKE

Preheat oven to 375°F.

TOPPING

COMBINE and blend well
- ¼ c. firmly packed brown sugar
- 1 tbs. soft butter
- 1 tbs. flour

ADD
- ¼ c. finely crushed graham crackers

Set aside

CAKE

MELT over hot (not boiling) water
- 1 6-oz. pkg. (1 c.) Semi-Sweet Chocolate Morsels

COMBINE and set aside
- 2½ c. finely crushed graham crackers
- ½ c. chopped pecans
- ¼ c. sifted flour
- 1 tsp. baking powder
- ½ tsp. baking soda
- ¼ tsp. salt

BLEND
- ½ c. firmly packed brown sugar
- ¼ c. butter

BEAT in
- 1 egg

ADD
- Crumb mixture alternately with
- 1 c. buttermilk

ADD
- Melted semi-sweet

Spread in greased 9" square pan

SPRINKLE over batter
- Topping

Press gently with spatula

BAKE at: 375°F.

TIME: 40 min.

Cut in approx. 2" squares

Serve warm, topped with whipped cream

YIELD: 16 servings

LUXURY LOAF

Preheat oven to 300°F.

MELT over hot (not boiling) water
- 1 6-oz. pkg. (1 c.) Semi-Sweet Chocolate Morsels

REMOVE from water

SIFT together and set aside
- 2 c. sifted flour
- 1 tsp. baking powder
- ½ tsp. salt

COMBINE and beat till creamy
- 1 c. butter or shortening
- 1 tsp. vanilla
- ¼ tsp. mace or nutmeg

BEAT in gradually
- 1 c. sugar

BEAT in, one at a time
- 5 eggs

STIR in
- Melted semi-sweet

ADD
- Flour mixture alternately with
- ¼ c. orange juice

FOLD in
- ¼ c. finely chopped nuts
- Grated rind, 1 orange

Pour in waxed paper-lined 10" x 5" x 3" pan

BAKE at: 300°F.

TIME: 1 hr. 40 min.

(See illustration 5)

page 14 / cakes

BROWN VELVET CAKE
Preheat oven to 375°F.

MELT over hot (not boiling) water
    1 6-oz. pkg. (1 c.) Semi-Sweet
      Chocolate Morsels
Remove from heat

SIFT together into large bowl
    1¾ c. sifted flour
    2½ tsp. baking powder
    1 tsp. Nescafé
    1 tsp. salt
    ½ tsp. baking soda

ADD and stir to blend
    1¼ c. firmly packed
      brown sugar
    1 c. buttermilk
    ½ c. soft shortening
    1½ tsp. vanilla
Beat 2 min. with electric mixer, at
medium speed, scraping bowl and
beaters as needed

ADD and beat 1 min. with mixer
    Melted semi-sweet
    ⅓ c. buttermilk
    1 egg
Line bottoms of two 8″ or 9″ layer
cake pans with waxed paper. Grease
sides of pans

Pour batter into prepared pans

BAKE at: 375°F.
TIME: 30 to 35 min.

Cool for 10 min., then remove from
pans
Cool

Fill and frost with Chocolate Butter
Frosting *(see page 23)*

DARK SECRET POUND CAKE
Preheat oven to 350°F.

MELT over hot (not boiling) water
    1 6-oz. pkg. (1 c.) Semi-Sweet
      Chocolate Morsels
Remove from heat; cool

SIFT together and set aside
    2½ c. sifted flour
    1 tsp. baking soda
    1 tsp. salt

COMBINE and beat till creamy
    1 c. sugar
    ⅔ c. soft butter

BLEND in
    Cooled semi-sweet

BEAT in, one at a time
    3 eggs

STIR in gradually
    Flour mixture
      alternately with
    ⅔ c. buttermilk
    1 tsp. vanilla

ADD and mix well
    ½ c. chopped walnuts
Pour into greased 10″ x 5″ x 3″ pan

BAKE at: 350°F.
TIME: approx 1 hr. and 10 min.

While hot, decorate with candied
cherries, angelica, almonds, etc.,
if desired

CHOCOLATE LAYER CAKE

Preheat oven to 325°F.

SIFT together and set aside
- 1¼ c. sifted flour
- 1¼ tsp. baking powder
- 1 tsp. salt

MELT over hot (not boiling) water
- 1 6-oz. pkg. (1 c.) Semi-Sweet Chocolate Morsels

Remove from water

ADD and stir till melted
- ⅔ c. shortening

COMBINE and beat till thick
- 3 egg yolks
- ¼ c. sugar
- 2 tsp. vanilla

STIR in
- Semi-sweet mixture

ADD and beat well
- ½ c. milk

STIR in
- Flour mixture

BEAT till stiff but not dry
- 3 egg whites

BEAT in gradually, and continue beating till stiff and glossy
- ¼ c. sugar

STIR gently into semi-sweet mixture
- Approx. ¼ egg-white mixture

FOLD in
- Remaining egg-white mixture

Pour into 2 greased and floured 8" layer cake pans

BAKE at: 325°F.

TIME: 25 to 30 min.

Remove from pans

Cool

Fill and frost with Speedy Chocolate Frosting *(see page 21)*

CHOCOLATE UPSIDE DOWN CAKE

Preheat oven to 350°F.

SPRINKLE into waxed paper-lined 8" square pan
- ½ c. chopped nuts

MELT over hot (not boiling) water
- 1 6-oz. pkg. (1 c.) Semi-Sweet Chocolate Morsels

ADD and beat till smooth
- 1 c. sifted confectioners' sugar
- ⅓ c. evaporated milk

Spread over nuts

SIFT together and set aside
- 1 c. plus 2 tbs. sifted flour
- 1½ tsp. baking powder
- ½ tsp. salt

COMBINE and beat till blended
- ¾ c. sugar
- ¼ c. soft shortening

BEAT in
- 1 egg

ADD and stir till smooth
- Flour mixture
  alternately with
- ½ c. milk
- 1 tsp. vanilla

Pour over chocolate mixture in pan

BAKE at: 350°F.

TIME: 45 to 50 min.

Let stand in pan 5 min. Invert on rack. Remove waxed paper. Cool Cut in 2" squares.

YIELD: 16 servings

page 16 / cakes

Cakes With a Festive Air

HOLIDAY FRUIT CAKE

This fruit cake says "happy holidays" for Christmas-tree trimming time, New Year's Day open houses, or when the family is home for Thanksgiving.

Preheat oven to 350°F.

SIFT together and set aside
  ½ c. sifted flour
  ½ tsp. baking powder
  ½ tsp. salt
  ¼ tsp. baking soda

MELT over hot (not boiling) water
  1 6-oz. pkg. (1 c.) Semi-Sweet
    Chocolate Morsels
Remove from water

COMBINE and beat till creamy
  ⅓ c. butter
  ¼ c. firmly packed brown sugar
  1 tsp. orange extract

BEAT in, one at a time
  3 eggs

STIR in
  Melted semi-sweet

ADD
  Flour mixture
    alternately with
  ¼ c. water

FOLD in
  1¾ c. mixed candied fruit,
    finely chopped
  1 c. finely chopped nuts

Pour into greased and floured
1½-qt. ring mold*

BAKE at: 350°F.

TIME: 35 min.
*Or for MINIATURE FRUIT CAKES

SPOON into greased 5-oz.
custard cups, using
  ⅓ c. for each

BAKE at: 350°F.

TIME: 35 min.

To decorate:

BRUSH hot cakes immediately with
  Corn syrup

ARRANGE in desired design on top
of cakes
  ¼ c. mixed candied fruit,
    coarsely chopped
  Nut halves

YIELD: 12

(See illustration 26)

PARTY BUTTERFLY CAKES

Have ready 24 cupcakes

Remove cone from top of each with knife. Cut cones in half, vertically

Prepare Butterscotch-Cream Cheese Frosting *(see page 24)*

FILL holes in cupcakes generously with
  Butterscotch-Cream Cheese
    Frosting

Press two halves of cones into Frosting to resemble "butterfly wings"

YIELD: 24

CALICO CRUMB CAKE

The Calico Cake is a favorite with small-fry: they love the look of it, almost as much as the taste.

Preheat oven to 350°F.

TOPPING

COMBINE and beat till creamy
- ½ c. firmly packed brown sugar
- ¼ c. soft butter
- ½ tsp. allspice

ADD and mix till crumbly; set aside
- ¾ c. sifted flour

CAKE

COMBINE and melt over hot (not boiling) water
- 1 6-oz. pkg. (1 c.) Semi-Sweet Chocolate Morsels
- ½ c. butter

Remove from water

SIFT together and set aside
- 2 c. sifted flour
- 1 tsp. baking soda
- ¾ tsp. salt

STIR into semi-sweet mixture
- 1 c. firmly packed brown sugar
- 1 tsp. vanilla

BEAT in, one at a time
- 2 eggs

ADD
- Flour mixture alternately with
- 1 c. buttermilk

Pour into greased 15" x 10" x 1" pan

SPRINKLE over top
- Topping
- ½ c. chopped nuts

BAKE at: 350°F.

TIME: 20 to 25 min.

YIELD: 15 approx. 3" squares

APPLESAUCE LOAF CAKE

Preheat oven to 350°F.

SIFT together and set aside
- 2 c. sifted flour
- 1 tsp. baking soda
- 1 tsp. salt

COMBINE and beat till creamy
- ¾ c. sugar
- ½ c. shortening
- 1 tsp. cinnamon
- 1 tsp. cloves
- ½ tsp. nutmeg

BEAT in, one at a time
- 2 eggs

ADD
- Flour mixture alternately with
- 1 c. canned applesauce

STIR in
- 1 6-oz. pkg. (1 c.) Semi-Sweet Chocolate Morsels
- ½ c. chopped nuts
- ½ c. raisins

Spread in waxed paper-lined 10" x 5" x 3" pan

BAKE at: 350°F.

TIME: 1 hr. 10 min.

Let stand 10 min. then remove from pan

Cool

To store: Wrap in foil and keep in a cool dry place or freeze

page 18 / cakes

Next we give you three aces to keep up your culinary sleeve for any kind of entertainment, and especially for all those card parties!

BUTTERSCOTCH DELIGHT LAYERS

Preheat oven to 375°F.

MELT over hot (not boiling) water
1 6-oz. pkg. (1 c.) Nestlé's
Butterscotch Morsels
Remove from water

SIFT together into large bowl
2½ c. sifted flour
3 tsp. baking powder
1½ tsp. salt
½ tsp. baking soda

ADD and mix till blended
1 c. firmly packed brown sugar
⅔ c. milk
⅓ c. soft butter
½ tsp. vanilla
Beat 2 min. by hand or at low speed on electric mixer

ADD and beat 2 min.
Melted butterscotch
⅓ c. milk
3 eggs
Pour into two lightly greased and floured 8″ or 9″ layer cake pans

BAKE at: 375°F.

TIME: 20 to 25 min.

Let cool on cake rack 10 min. Remove from pans and cool thoroughly

Fill and frost with Butterscotch Delight Frosting *(see page 24)*

HAWAIIAN PINEAPPLE CAKE FOR A CROWD

Preheat oven to 375°F.

TOPPING

COMBINE and set aside
1 c. flaked coconut
½ c. canned, crushed pineapple, undrained

CAKE

SIFT together and set aside
2 c. sifted flour
1 tsp. baking powder
½ tsp. baking soda
¼ tsp. salt

COMBINE and beat till creamy
¾ c. sugar
½ c. shortening
Dash ginger

BEAT in, one at a time
2 eggs

ADD
Flour mixture
alternately with
¾ c. canned, crushed pineapple, undrained

ADD
1 6-oz. pkg. (1 c.) Semi-Sweet Chocolate Morsels
Spread in greased
15″ x 10″ x 1″ pan

SPRINKLE evenly over top
Topping

BAKE at: 375°F.

TIME: 25 min.

Cool. Cut in 3″ x 2″ pieces

YIELD: 25 servings
(See illustration 21)

MARDI GRAS PARTY CAKE

Preheat oven to 375°F.

MELT in saucepan
- ⅔ 6-oz. pkg. (⅔ c.) Butterscotch Morsels
- ¼ c. water

Cool

SIFT together and set aside
- 2¼ c. sifted flour
- 1 tsp. salt
- 1 tsp. baking soda
- ½ tsp. baking powder

COMBINE and beat till creamy
- 1¼ c. sugar
- ½ c. shortening

BEAT in, one at a time
- 3 eggs

BLEND in
- Melted butterscotch mixture

ADD
- Dry ingredients alternately with
- 1 c. buttermilk

Pour into two greased and floured 9″ layer cake pans

BAKE at: 375°F.

TIME: 25 to 30 min.

Cool

FILLING

COMBINE in saucepan
- ½ c. sugar
- ½ c. evaporated milk
- ⅓ c. Butterscotch Morsels
- ⅓ c. water
- 1 tbs. cornstarch

ADD and cook over medium heat, stirring till thick
- 1 egg yolk, beaten

Remove from heat

ADD
- 1 c. flaked coconut
- 1 c. chopped pecans
- 2 tbs. butter

Cool. Spread between layers and on top to within ½″ of edge. Frost sides and top edge with seven minute frosting or whipped cream
(See illustration 6)

COCONUT MARBLE FUDGE CAKE
COCONUT MIXTURE

COMBINE and beat till foamy
  1 egg white
  1 tbs. water
  1 tsp. vanilla

BEAT in gradually and continue
beating till stiff, glossy peaks form
  ½ c. sugar

FOLD in and set aside
  2 c. (1 7-oz pkg.)
    packaged grated coconut
  1 tbs. flour
  ¼ tsp. salt

CAKE MIXTURE

Preheat oven to 350°F.

COMBINE in saucepan and stir over
moderate heat till semi-sweet melts
  1 6-oz. pkg. (1 c.) Semi-Sweet
    Chocolate Morsels
  ½ c. water
  1 tsp. Nescafé

Remove from water

SIFT together and set aside
  2 c. sifted flour
  1 tsp. baking soda

BEAT till foamy
  3 egg whites

BEAT in gradually, and continue
beating till stiff, glossy peaks form
  6 tbs. sugar

COMBINE and beat till creamy
  1 c. sugar
  ½ c. soft shortening
  3 egg yolks
  1 tsp. vanilla
  ½ tsp. salt

ADD
  Flour mixture
    alternately with
  Semi-sweet mixture
  ½ c. sour cream

FOLD in
  Egg white mixture

POUR into 9″ or 10″ tube pan,
greased on bottom
  ⅓ of Cake Mixture

SPOON over
  ½ of Coconut Mixture

Repeat layers like this and top with
remaining Cake Mixture

BAKE at: 350°F.

TIME: approx. 1 hr.

Cool cake (right side-up) for at
least ½ hour before removing
from pan

Invert on serving plate and frost
with Luscious Chocolate Frosting
(see page 21)

Frostings, Fillings and Glazes

Here are the frostings, fillings, and glazes that will transform your cake into the delectable *pièce de résistance* of any meal you serve. Whip them up at a moment's notice to turn the most unexpected visit into a festive occasion.

SPEEDY CHOCOLATE FROSTING

COMBINE in saucepan
    ½ c. evaporated milk
    Dash salt
Bring *just* to boil over moderate heat, stirring constantly

ADD and stir till chocolate melts and mixture is smooth
    1 6-oz. pkg. (1 c.) Semi-Sweet Chocolate Morsels
    1 tsp. vanilla
Cool till thick enough to spread
Frosts two 8″ layers or one 13″ x 9″ cake

LUSCIOUS CHOCOLATE FROSTING

COMBINE in saucepan and bring *just* to boil over moderate heat, stirring constantly
    ¼ c. butter
    ¼ c. milk
Remove from heat

ADD and stir till melted and smooth
    1 6-oz. pkg. (1 c.) Semi-Sweet Chocolate Morsels

STIR in
    1 egg yolk
    1 tsp. vanilla

BEAT in gradually
    2 c. sifted confectioners' sugar
Continue beating till stiff enough to spread
Fills and frosts two 8″ or 9″ cake layers

CHOCOLATE FILLING AND GLAZE

BASIC
MELT over hot (not boiling) water
    1 6-oz. pkg. (1 c.) Semi-Sweet Chocolate Morsels
Remove from water

STIR in till smooth
    ½ c. light corn syrup
    2 tbs. water

GLAZE
RESERVE for use as Glaze
    ¼ c. semi-sweet mixture

FILLING
FOLD into the remaining semi-sweet mixture
    1 c. heavy cream, whipped
    1 tsp. vanilla
Nice to fill and glaze cream puffs or dessert shells

page 22 | *cakes*

CHOCOLATE CREAM FROSTING

COMBINE in small saucepan and stir over low heat till well blended
- ½ 6-oz. pkg. (½ c.) Semi-Sweet Chocolate Morsels
- 2 tbs. honey
- 1 tbs. water

Remove from heat. Cool till slightly thickened

COMBINE and beat till thick
- 1½ c. heavy cream
- ⅛ tsp. Nescafé
- ⅛ tsp. salt

FOLD in gently till well blended
- Semi-sweet mixture

Fills and frosts two or three 8″ or 9″ cake layers

Chill frosted cake before serving
(See illustrations 7, 23)

CHOCOLATE FONDANT GLAZE

COMBINE and bring *just* to boil over moderate heat, stirring constantly
- 2 tbs. shortening
- ¼ c. light corn syrup
- 3 tbs. water

Remove from heat

STIR in till smooth
- 1 6-oz. pkg. (1 c.) Semi-Sweet Chocolate Morsels

Cool 2 to 3 min. till thick enough to spread

Will frost 1 10″ sponge or angel food cake
(See illustrations 4, 23)

EASY CHOCOLATE FROSTING

COMBINE and bring *just* to boil over moderate heat, stirring constantly
- 1 14-oz. can (1¼ c.) sweetened condensed milk
- ¼ c. butter
- ¼ tsp. salt

Boil 1 min., stirring constantly

Remove from heat

ADD and stir till blended and smooth
- 1 6-oz. pkg. (1 c.) Semi-Sweet Chocolate Morsels
- 1 tsp. vanilla

Cool about 20 min. — till thick enough to spread

Fills and frosts two 8″ or 9″ cake layers

CHOCOLATE VELVET FROSTING

MELT over hot (not boiling) water
- 1½ 6-oz. pkgs. (1½ c.) Semi-Sweet Chocolate Morsels
- 3 tbs. shortening

Remove from heat

ADD and beat till smooth
- ½ c. sifted confectioners' sugar
- ½ c. evaporated milk
- 2 tsp. vanilla
- ¼ tsp. salt

Let stand till set

Fills and frosts two 8″ or 9″ cake layers

QUIK CHOCOLATE FROSTING

COMBINE and stir till smooth
- 1 c. Nestlé's Chocolate Quik
- ¼ c. soft butter
- 1 tsp. vanilla
- ¼ c. boiling water

BEAT in gradually till smooth and thick enough to spread
- 2¾ c. sifted confectioners' sugar

Fills and frosts two 8" cake layers

Other uses: Press through pastry tube to decorate cookies or frosted cake

COCOA CREAM FROSTING

COMBINE in small bowl
- 1 c. chilled, heavy cream
- ¼ c. Nestlé's EverReady Cocoa
- ¼ c. firmly packed brown sugar

Beat till thick enough to hold its shape

Use to frost cakes* or as topping on desserts

YIELD: approx. 2 c.

*When used as cake frosting, chill before serving
(See illustration 23)

GLOSSY CHOCOLATE FROSTING

COMBINE in saucepan and bring *just* to boil over moderate heat, stirring constantly
- ¼ c. light corn syrup
- 3 tbs. water
- 2 tbs. shortening

Remove from heat

ADD and stir till melted and smooth
- 1 6-oz. pkg. (1 c.) Semi-Sweet Chocolate Morsels

ADD
- 1 tsp. vanilla

BLEND in gradually
- 2 c. sifted confectioners' sugar

Fills and frosts two 8" or 9" cake layers or 24 cupcakes

CHOCOLATE BUTTER FROSTING

COMBINE and bring *just* to boil over moderate heat, stirring constantly
- ⅓ c. milk
- ¼ c. butter

Remove from heat

STIR in till smooth
- 1 6-oz. pkg. (1 c.) Semi-Sweet Chocolate Morsels
- 1 tsp. vanilla

BEAT in gradually till thick enough to spread
- 2¼ c. sifted confectioners' sugar

Fills and frosts two 8" or 9" cake layers

EASY EVERREADY FROSTING

COMBINE in small mixing bowl and beat till stiff enough to spread
- 2½ c. sifted confectioners' sugar
- 1½ c. Nestlé's EverReady Cocoa
- ¼ c. soft butter
- ¼ c. boiling water
- 1 tsp. vanilla
- ⅛ tsp. salt

Fills and frosts two 8" or 9" layers

BUTTERSCOTCH DELIGHT FROSTING

MELT over hot (not boiling) water
1 6-oz. pkg. (1 c.)
   Butterscotch Morsels

ADD and stir till blended
2 tbs. water

Remove from heat

Cool to lukewarm

COMBINE and beat till light
1 8-oz. pkg. cream cheese
1 tbs. light cream
⅛ tsp. salt

BLEND in
Melted butterscotch
1 tsp. vanilla

FOLD in
1 c. heavy cream, whipped

Fills and frosts two 8″ or 9″
cake layers

BUTTERSCOTCH BUTTER FROSTING

MELT over hot (not boiling) water
1 6-oz. pkg. (1 c.)
   Butterscotch Morsels

Remove from water

ADD and stir till smooth
⅓ c. milk
2 tbs. butter
⅛ tsp. salt

BEAT in gradually, then beat till
thick enough to spread
3 c. (approx.) sifted
   confectioners' sugar

Fills and frosts two 8″ or 9″ layers
(See illustration 23)

CREAMY BUTTERSCOTCH FROSTING

MELT over hot (not boiling) water
1 6-oz. pkg. (1 c.)
   Butterscotch Morsels

ADD and stir till blended
1 tbs. water

Remove from water

COMBINE and beat till creamy
1 8-oz. pkg. soft cream cheese
⅛ tsp. salt

ADD and stir till smooth
Melted butterscotch

BEAT in gradually, then beat till
thick enough to spread
3 c. sifted confectioners' sugar

Fills and frosts two 8″ or 9″ layers.
Chill till ready to serve

BUTTERSCOTCH-CREAM CHEESE FROSTING

COMBINE over low heat and stir
till blended
1 6-oz. pkg. (1 c.)
   Butterscotch Morsels
4 tbs. honey
2 tbs. water

Remove from heat. Cool

COMBINE and beat till fluffy
1 8-oz. pkg. cream cheese
¼ tsp. salt

BLEND in
Butterscotch mixture

COMBINE and beat till thick
1½ c. heavy cream
⅛ tsp. Nescafé

FOLD in gently, till well blended
Butterscotch mixture

Fills and frosts two 8″ or 9″
layer cakes
Chill till ready to serve

CHOCOLATE BUTTER-CREAM FILLING

BLEND at high speed in electric blender for 6 seconds
- ½ 6-oz. pkg. (½ c.) Semi-Sweet Chocolate Morsels

ADD and blend on high speed for 6 seconds
- 2 tbs. boiling water

ADD and blend on high speed for 15 seconds or till smooth
- ¼ c. soft butter
- 2 egg yolks
- 2 tbs. confectioners' sugar
- 1 tbs. rum

Fills an 8" or 9" layer cake

FLUFFY MARBLE FROSTING

COMBINE and stir over low heat till smooth
- 1 6-oz. pkg. (1 c.) Semi-Sweet Chocolate Morsels
- 3 tbs. light corn syrup
- 1 tbs. water

Remove from heat.

PREPARE according to label directions
- 1 pkg. fluffy white frosting mix

POUR over fluffy frosting
- Semi-sweet mixture

Fold once or twice with spatula. (As frosting is spread on cake it will marbleize)

Fills and frosts two 8" or 9" cake layers

FUDGE FROSTING

COMBINE and bring to a *full* boil over moderate heat, stirring constantly
- ½ c. evaporated milk
- ½ c. sugar
- 2 tbs. butter
- ⅛ tsp. salt

Boil 5 min., over moderate heat, stirring occasionally

Remove from heat

ADD at once stirring till blended and smooth
- 1 6-oz. pkg. (1 c.) Semi-Sweet Chocolate Morsels

BEAT in
- 2 tbs. light corn syrup

Cool till thick enough to spread — approx. 15 min.

Fills and frosts two 8" or 9" cake layers

(See illustration 1)

SOUR CREAM VELVET FROSTING

MELT over hot (not boiling) water. Stir till smooth
- 1 6-oz. pkg. (1 c.) Semi-Sweet Chocolate Morsels

Remove from water

BLEND in
- ½ c. sour cream
- 1 tsp. vanilla
- ¼ tsp. salt

BEAT in gradually
- 2½ c. sifted confectioners' sugar

Fills and frosts two 8" or 9" cake layers

page 26 / cakes

STRAWBERRY BUTTER FROSTING

DISSOLVE
　1 to 2 tbs. Nestlé's
　　Strawberry Quik*
　　in
　3 tbs. milk

COMBINE and beat till creamy
　1 c. sifted confectioners' sugar
　⅓ c. soft butter
　⅛ tsp. salt

ADD gradually
　2 c. sifted confectioners' sugar
　　alternately with
　Quik mixture

Fills and frosts two 8″ or 9″ layers

Other uses: Press through pastry tube to decorate cookies or frosted cakes

*according to color desired

BUTTER-CHOC FROSTING

COMBINE and bring *just* to boil over moderate heat, stirring constantly
　½ c. evaporated milk
　Dash salt
Remove from heat

STIR in till smooth
　1 6-oz. pkg. (1 c.) Semi-Sweet
　　Chocolate Morsels
　⅓ 6-oz. pkg. (⅓ c.)
　　Butterscotch Morsels

Cool to room temperature or till thick enough to spread

Fills and frosts two 9″ cake layers

FLUFFY STRAWBERRY FROSTING

COMBINE and bring to boil stirring till Quik is dissolved
　½ c. water
　¼ c. Nestlé's Strawberry Quik

ADD and beat at low speed on electric mixer till well blended
　Contents of 1 pkg. fluffy
　　white frosting mix

Continue beating at high speed till stiff peaks form

Fills and frosts two 8″ or 9″ cake layers

(See illustration 23)

You can become a skilled cake decorator in a few minutes, once you've learned the tricks of the trade. Part of the skill lies in the practiced hand — your cakes will look better and better as you gain experience—but most of it depends on knowing the expert's little secrets, the techniques that give cake decoration a professional touch. Why not stage your own "cake decorating clinic" and try these new, simplified ideas?

MORSEL MAGIC

Semi-Sweet Chocolate Morsels, just as they are, add a decorator's note to many a cake. Press them into the frosting, points down, to ornament the top and sides of a cake with gay polka dots. . . . *Black and Tan:* For a stylish effect, cover the cake with butterscotch frosting, made with Butterscotch Morsels, and trim it with the chocolate polka dots. . . . *Name Day:* Say happy birthday to a child by sticking the morsels, points down, side by side into his birthday cake frosting to spell his name. . . . *Borderline Cake:* Set the morsels, points up, around the top or base of the cake to make an attractive border.

CLASSIC FEATHERED DESIGN

Frost cake with white frosting. Melt ¼ cup Semi-Sweet Chocolate Morsels and ½ teaspoon vegetable shortening over hot (not boiling) water. Force chocolate mixture through narrow opening of decorating tube at 1-inch intervals across top of cake. Using a small wooden pick, lightly cross chocolate lines at 1-inch intervals, "feathering" across top of cake.

(See illustration 23)

Decorator's hint: To achieve evenly spaced, parallel lines of chocolate, guide yourself by marking the frosting at regular intervals. Do this by holding a thin thread taut, and pressing it into the frosting.

FESTIVE CHOCOLATE SILHOUETTES

Melt ½ 6-ounce package (½ cup) Semi-Sweet Chocolate Morsels and ½ teaspoon vegetable shortening over hot (not boiling) water. Spread the melted chocolate in a thin, even layer on waxed paper. Place on a cookie sheet. Chill until firm. Invert on wax paper. Carefully peel off top paper. Cut out silhouettes with small cookie cutters or paper patterns. Place silhouettes, as desired, on cakes or cup cakes frosted in white or pale colors.

(See illustration 3)

Decorator's hint: The prettiest silhouettes are the ones you design yourself. Cut patterns out of stiff paper—a heart for Valentine's Day, a hatchet for Washington's Birthday, a tulip or a rabbit for Easter, or whatever suits the special occasion. Lay the pattern on the chocolate and use a sharp knife point to cut carefully around the edges.

page 28 | cakes

CHOCOLATE CREAM CROWN

Melt ¾ 6-ounce package (¾ cup) Semi-Sweet Chocolate Morsels over hot (not boiling) water. Remove from heat. Add ⅓ cup light corn syrup and 1 tablespoon water, stir until smooth; cool. Whip 1 cup heavy cream with 1 teaspoon vanilla until stiff. Fold in semi-sweet mixture. Fill and frost top and sides of two 8- or 9-inch cake layers. Alternate peaks of frosting with walnut halves around top rim of cake. To form peaks, force frosting through pastry tube. Top frosting peaks with ¼ 6-ounce package (¼ cup) Semi-Sweet Chocolate Morsels.

Decorator's hint: Frost the sides of your cake first, using a spatula or rubber scraper and holding it vertically to spread the frosting from bottom to top. Then place a good quantity of frosting on the center of the cake top and spread it evenly to the edges. To keep your cake plate free of frosting, cut a square of waxed paper in half, place the pieces on the plate side by side before you frost the cake, and pull them out in opposite directions when you have finished frosting the cake.

Flavor hint: For a change of flavor and a nice golden tan look on your cake, follow the directions above, substituting Butterscotch Morsels for Semi-Sweet Chocolate Morsels.

CAROL CAKE

Frost loaf cake with white frosting. Melt ½ cup Semi-Sweet Chocolate Morsels over hot (not boiling) water. Force melted chocolate through decorating tube to make a musical staff on top of cake. Dot staff and sides of cake with additional morsels, points in, to form bases of musical notes. With decorating tube make stems of notes. Place row of Semi-Sweet Chocolate Morsels around base of cake.

Decorator's hint: If you have no decorating tube, you can make one by cutting out a triangle of stiff white paper, rolling it into a hollow cone, secured with Scotch tape, and snipping off the pointed end.

CHOCOLATE SHADOW GLAZE

Frost sides of cake with white or pastel frosting. Melt ½ 6-ounce package (½ cup) Semi-Sweet Chocolate Morsels over hot (not boiling) water. Remove from water; add ¼ cup light corn syrup and 1 teaspoon water. Stir until smooth; cool to room temperature. Spread chocolate glaze over top of cake, allowing some to drizzle down sides over frosting.

Decorator's hint: To make attractively spaced "drizzles" down the sides of the cake, use a knife or a spoon to push small amounts of the glaze over the edge at desired intervals. The length of the "drizzle" will depend on the amount you push.

Color hint: Make pastel frostings —pink, yellow, or pale green—by adding a few drops of vegetable coloring to your frosting mixture. The dark chocolate shadow looks strikingly handsome against the pastel shades.

HIDDEN TREASURE CAKE

The secret of the Hidden Treasure Cake is an inside story. Start with an angel food cake—you can buy it, or make it with a mix. The chocolate filling is the heart of the cake, hiding in readiness to give everyone a happy surprise when the cake is cut.

(See illustration 4)

Combine ½ pound (32) marshmallows, ¼ teaspoon salt, and ⅓ cup water in saucepan; place over medium heat until melted, stirring constantly. Remove from heat. Stir in 1 6-ounce package (1 cup) Semi-Sweet Chocolate Morsels until melted. Chill approximately 10 minutes. Fold in 1 cup heavy cream, whipped, and ⅛ teaspoon almond extract. Cut a slice about 1 inch thick from the top of 1 10-inch angel food cake. Set aside. Gently hollow out a trench in remaining cake 2 inches wide and 2 inches deep — a grapefruit knife does this job well. Tear cake pieces slightly. Fill trench with half the filling. Place torn cake on top; press down slightly. Top with remaining filling. Replace top of cake. Chill several hours.

Note: If desired, sides of cake may be frosted with ½ cup heavy cream whipped with ¼ cup Nestlé's Chocolate Quik.

TUNNEL OF LOVE CAKE

The Tunnel of Love Cake is our Hidden Treasure Cake with a special Valentine's Day decoration. Assemble a bouquet of sweetheart roses, wiring it together to keep its shape intact. Set it over the center of the cake, with the stems descending into the hole. What could be lovelier, or more loving?

The Very Best Cookies

Every homemaker is constantly on the alert for bright new ideas in the cookie department. PERFECT ENDINGS presents an unusual collection of old favorites brought up to date as well as brand new ones.

The cookie recipes we have gathered here were sparked by a fortunate experiment when an imaginative New England homemaker dropped morsels of semi-sweet chocolate into cookie dough prepared according to a treasured recipe. The result, Toll House Cookies, made culinary history. Unlike all other baking chocolate, the morsels stayed whole during the entire baking period. Housewives welcomed this new sensation with delight. Semi-Sweet Chocolate Morsels revolutionized preparation techniques, simplified mixing and blending, and made possible countless time-saving short-cuts. You will find these benefits reflected in the recipes that follow.

The delicious flavor, the satisfying texture, the *goodness* have made Toll House an all-time favorite. They opened the door not only to a new era in cookie-baking, but also to a whole wonderful world of semi-sweet creative cookery.

This chapter will be of special interest to teenagers, for cookies are high on their lists of snacks, desserts, good gifts, and party treats. PERFECT ENDINGS gives you a wide selection of cookies to choose from: butter cookies, meringues, drop, molded, and sliced cookies, bars and squares. You—and your family—will find enjoyment both in the making and in the eating. We hope that the recipes in this chapter will help you retain and pass on to your daughters that priceless ingredient—a love of good cooking.

Toll House Cookies

ORIGINAL TOLL HOUSE® COOKIES

Preheat oven to 375°F.

SIFT together and set aside
- 1 c. plus 2 tbs. sifted flour
- ½ tsp. baking soda
- ½ tsp. salt

BLEND
- ½ c. soft butter or shortening
- 6 tbs. granulated sugar
- 6 tbs. brown sugar
- ½ tsp. vanilla
- ¼ tsp. water

BEAT in
- 1 egg

ADD and mix well
- Flour mixture

STIR in
- 1 6-oz. pkg. (1 c.) Nestlé's Semi-Sweet Chocolate Morsels
- ½ c. coarsely chopped nuts

Drop by well-rounded half teaspoonfuls on greased cookie sheet

BAKE at: 375°F.

TIME: 10 to 12 min.

YIELD: 50 cookies

SUBSTITUTION FOR NUTS

Substitute *one* of the following for nuts:

RAISINS
- 1 c. chopped raisins
  and
- 1 tsp. grated orange rind

DATES
- 1 c. chopped dates

PRUNES AND APRICOTS
- ½ c. dried prunes, pitted and coarsely chopped
  and
- ½ c. dried apricots, coarsely chopped

CANDIED FRUIT
- 1 c. mixed candied fruit, finely chopped
  and
- ½ tsp. orange extract (optional)

CORNFLAKES
- 2 c. cornflakes, uncrushed

BAKE at: 375°F.

TIME: 8 to 10 min.

(See illustration 13)

Variations:

1. COOKIE POPS

Drop by tablespoonfuls 4 inches apart on greased cookie sheet. Flatten slightly with back of spoon. Insert 5-inch lollipop sticks—push sticks from edge to about two-thirds through batter

BAKE at 375°F. 10 to 12 min. Remove gently while warm with wide spatula. Let cool thoroughly before serving

YIELD: approx. 1½ dozen (3″ cookies)

(continued on page 32)

page 32 / cookies

(continued from page 31)

2. ICE CREAM SANDWICHES

Have ready cooled Toll House Cookies

Set control of refrigerator at coldest point

SPREAD softened vanilla ice cream between two cookies. Wrap for freezing. Freeze till ready to serve

HOW TO MAIL TOLL HOUSE COOKIES

Wrap two cooled cookies back-to-back in aluminum foil. Stand on end and pack in rows in box. The foil acts as a shock absorber and prevents the cookies from crumbling

HOW TO FRESHEN TOLL HOUSE COOKIES

Wrap cookies in aluminum foil. Place in 375°F. oven for 5 min.

TOLL HOUSE MARBLE SQUARES

Preheat oven to 375°F.

SIFT together and set aside
  1 c. plus 2 tbs. sifted flour*
  ½ tsp. baking soda
  ½ tsp. salt

BLEND
  ½ c. soft butter
    (or shortening)
  6 tbs. granulated sugar
  6 tbs. firmly packed brown sugar
  ½ tsp. vanilla
  ¼ tsp. water

BEAT in
  1 egg

ADD and mix well
  Flour mixture

STIR in
  ½ c. coarsely chopped nuts

Spread in greased 13″ x 9″ x 2″ pan

SPRINKLE over top of batter
  1 6-oz. pkg. (1 c.) Semi-Sweet Chocolate Morsels**

Place in 375°F. oven 1 min.

Remove from oven and run knife through batter to marbleize

Return to oven and continue to bake

BAKE at: 375°F.

TIME: 12 to 14 min.

Cool

Cut in 2″ squares

                    YIELD: 2 dozen

To make TOLL HOUSE

OATMEAL MARBLE SQUARES:

  *Reduce flour to ¾ c.
  **Add 1 c. rolled oats

"EASY-TO-MAKE" TOLL HOUSE MARBLE SQUARES

Preheat oven to 375°F.

Prepare "Easy-to-Make" Drop Cookie dough, according to directions on package of Nestlés All Purpose Cookie Mix

STIR in
  ½ c. chopped nuts

Spread in greased 13″ x 9″ x 2″ pan

SPRINKLE over top of cookie dough
  1 6-oz. pkg. (1 c.) Semi-Sweet Chocolate Morsels

Place in oven 2 min. Remove from oven and run knife through batter to marbleize. Return to oven

BAKE at: 375°F.

TIME: 10 to 12 min.

Cool. Cut into 2″ squares

                    YIELD: 2 dozen

1   America's all-time favorite: yellow layer cake swirled with Fudge Frosting (p. 25)—a truly satisfying "perfect ending."

2   The New Orleans Torte (p. 124) is layered and topped with creamy chocolate-cream cheese filling-frosting, and trimmed with colorful candy sprinkles. Try serving it with a beautiful bowl of Hot Tea Punch (p. 178).

3   A card party conversation-piece is this Devil's Food Cake (p. 10) with a fluffy white frosting. Decorate the top with easy-to-make Chocolate Silhouettes (p. 27).

4   Chilled chocolate filling forms the center of our Hidden Treasure Cake (p. 29). Topped with the richness of Chocolate Fondant Glaze (p. 22), it's a treat your guests—and your family—will rave about.

5   Treats for teatime. Serve this Luxury Loaf (p. 13)—topped with nut clusters—and Oriental Brittle "Cookies" (p. 66), with bracing cups of Hot Tea Toddy (p. 177).

6   It's sure to be a happy birthday when you bite into this gala masterpiece—Mardi Gras Party Cake (p. 19). For the nibblers, set out bowls of Mocha Coconut Patties (p. 141) and Nescafé Glazed Pecans (p. 143).

7   Any time is party-time when the dessert is a Swiss Chocolate Cake (p. 10). Its luscious Chocolate Cream Frosting (p. 22) is the perfect crowning touch for this culinary masterpiece.

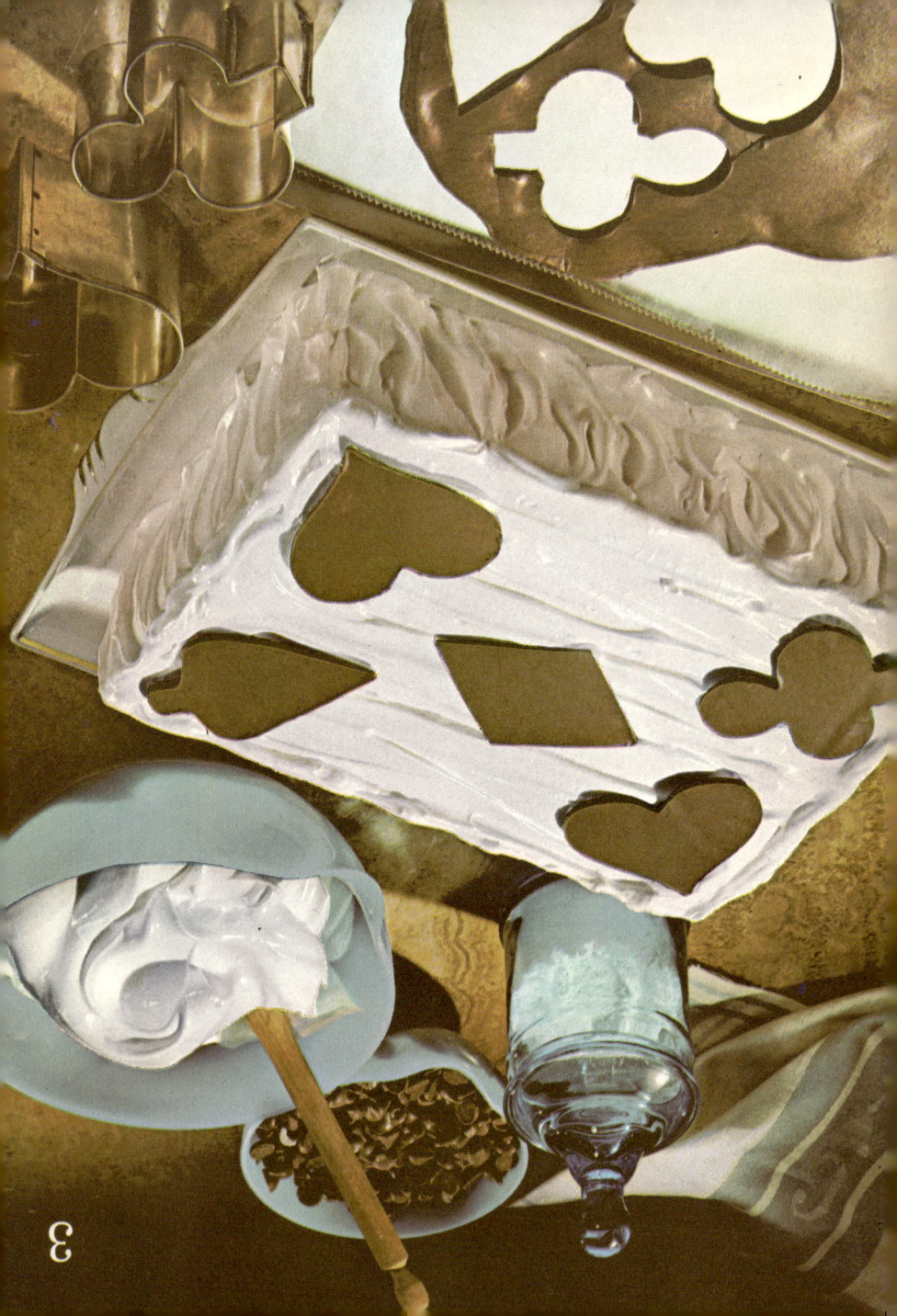

4

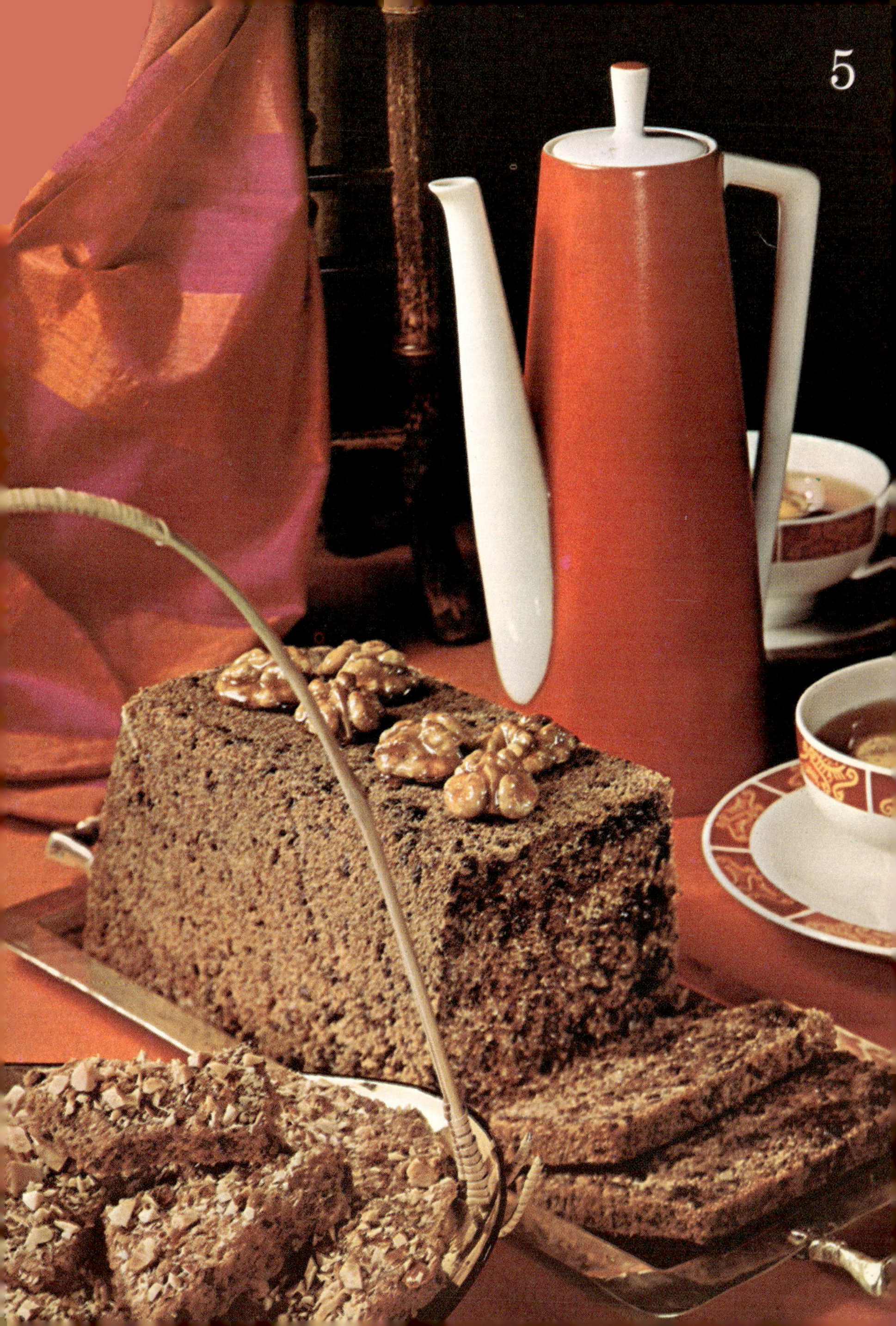

5

6

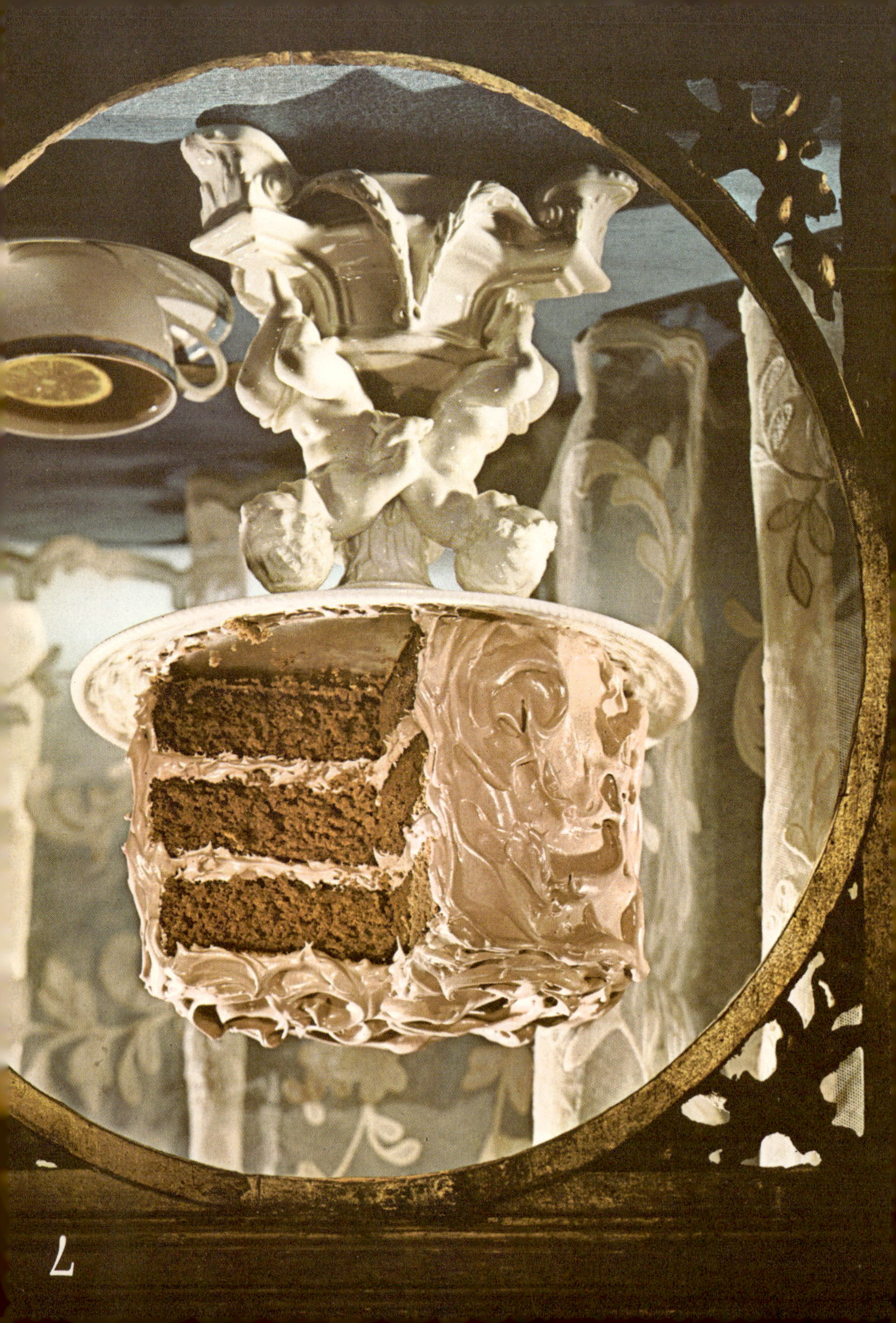

L

Extra-Delicious Bar Cookies

Bars, according to a Webster of the baking oven, are a combination of cookie and cake, combining the best features of each. They have the appetite-satisfaction of cake, with the convenience of a cookie.

FUDGE BROWNIES

Preheat oven to 325°F.

SIFT together and set aside
    ¾ c. sifted flour
    ¼ tsp. baking soda
    ¼ tsp. salt

COMBINE and bring *just* to boil, stirring constantly
    ½ c. sugar
    ⅓ c. vegetable shortening
    2 tbs. water

Remove from heat

ADD and stir till blended
    1 6-oz. pkg. (1 c.) Semi-Sweet Chocolate Morsels
    1 tsp. vanilla

BEAT in, one at a time
    2 eggs

STIR in
    Flour mixture
    ½ c. coarsely chopped nuts

Spread in greased 9″ square pan
BAKE at: 325°F.
TIME: 25 min.
YIELD: 16

(See illustration 14)

NUT MALLOW BROWNIES

Preheat oven to 350°F.

MELT over hot (not boiling) water
    1 6-oz. pkg. (1 c.) Semi-Sweet Chocolate Morsels

Remove from heat

SIFT together and set aside
    1 c. sifted flour
    ½ tsp. baking soda
    ½ tsp. salt

COMBINE and beat till creamy
    ¾ c. sugar
    ½ c. shortening
    2 eggs

BLEND in
    Melted semi-sweet

STIR in
    Flour mixture
    1 tsp. vanilla

ADD
    ¾ c. chopped nuts

Spread in greased 9″ square pan
BAKE at: 350°F.
TIME: approx. 25 min.

TOP immediately with
    24 marshmallows, cut in quarters

MELT over hot (not boiling) water
    1 6-oz. pkg. (1 c.) Semi-Sweet Chocolate Morsels
    1 tbs. shortening

Spoon over marshmallows
Cool
YIELD: 25 squares

page 42 / cookies

POLKA DOT SQUARES

Preheat oven to 400°F.

MELT in large saucepan
⅔ c. butter or shortening

STIR in
2¼ c. firmly packed
brown sugar
Remove from heat —
cool approx. 10 min.

SIFT together and set aside
2⅔ c. sifted flour
2½ tsp. baking powder
1 tsp. salt

ADD to sugar mixture and beat
till smooth
3 eggs

ADD and mix well
Flour mixture
1 c. nuts, chopped
2 6-oz. pkgs. or 1 12-oz.
pkg. (2 c.) Semi-Sweet
Chocolate Morsels
Spread in greased
15″ x 10″ x 1″ pan

BAKE at: 400°F.

TIME: 18 min.

Cool. Cut in 2″ squares

YIELD: approx. 3 dozen

CHOCO-NUT DREAM BARS

Preheat oven to 350°F.

COOKIE

COMBINE and beat till blended
⅔ c. sugar
½ c. soft butter
½ tsp. vanilla
¼ tsp. salt

STIR in gradually
1 c. sifted flour

Press over bottom of ungreased 13″
x 9″ x 2″ pan

BAKE at: 350°F.

TIME: approx. 16 to 18 min.

Cool 5 min.

Cover with

TOPPING

COMBINE and beat till light
1 c. sugar
2 eggs
1 tsp. vanilla
¾ tsp. salt

ADD and stir to blend well
3 c. finely chopped nuts
Spread over cooled, baked layer

BAKE at: 350°F.

TIME: 20 min.

Cool, frost with

FROSTING

COMBINE and bring *just* to boil
over moderate heat
½ c. evaporated milk
Dash salt

ADD and stir till smooth
1 6-oz. pkg. (1 c.) Semi-Sweet
Chocolate Morsels
1 tsp. vanilla
Cool till thick enough to spread —
approx. 5 min.

Spread over top of baked mixture

Cool, cut in 2″ x 1″ bars

YIELD: approx. 48 bars

EASY POLKA DOT SQUARES

Preheat oven to 350°F.

COMBINE
- 2 c. graham cracker crumbs
- 1 14-oz. can (1¼ c.) sweetened condensed milk
- 1 6-oz. pkg. (1 c.) Semi-Sweet Chocolate Morsels
- 1 tsp. vanilla
- ½ tsp. salt

ADD
- 1 8-oz pkg. dates, chopped (approx. 1¼ c.)

Press into a greased 8″ square pan

BAKE at: 350°F.

TIME: 35 min.

Cool

Cut into 1¼″ squares

YIELD: 36

CHOCO-NUT DELIGHTS

Preheat oven to 350°F.

SIFT together and set aside
- 1¼ c. sifted flour
- ½ tsp. baking soda
- ½ tsp. salt

COMBINE and beat till creamy
- ½ c. soft butter
- ½ c. firmly packed brown sugar
- ¼ c. granulated sugar
- ½ tsp. vanilla
- ¼ tsp. water

BEAT in
- 1 egg

STIR in and mix well
- Flour mixture

Spread in ungreased 13″ x 9″ x 2″ pan

BAKE at: 350°F.

TIME: 15 min.

SPRINKLE at once with
- 1 6-oz. pkg. (1 c.) Semi-Sweet Chocolate Morsels

Let stand 2 min. to melt, then spread to cover top

COMBINE over hot (not boiling) water
- 1 6-oz. pkg. (1 c.) Semi-Sweet Chocolate Morsels
- ⅓ c. maple-blended syrup
- 2 tbs. butter
- 1 tsp. vanilla
- ¼ tsp. salt

STIR in
- 2 c. coarsely chopped pecans

SPREAD evenly over Semi-sweet layer

BAKE at: 350°F.

TIME: 8 min.

Cool

Cut in 1½″ x 1″ bars

YIELD: 64 bars

CRUNCHY FUDGE BARS

Preheat oven to 350°F.

COOKIE MIXTURE

SIFT together and set aside
   ¾ c. sifted flour
   ½ tsp. baking soda
   ½ tsp. salt

COMBINE and beat till creamy
   1 c. firmly packed brown sugar
   ½ c. shortening
   1 egg
   ½ tsp. vanilla

BLEND in gradually
   Flour mixture

STIR in
   1 c. crushed cornflakes
   1 c. quick-cooking rolled oats
   ½ c. chopped nuts

REMOVE and reserve
   1 c. dough, firmly packed

PRESS into greased 9″ square pan
   Remaining dough
Prepare

FUDGE FILLING

MELT over hot (not boiling) water
   1 6-oz. pkg. (1 c.) Semi-Sweet
      Chocolate Morsels
   1 tbs. shortening
Remove from heat

ADD and stir to blend
   1 c. finely chopped nuts
   ⅓ c. sweetened condensed milk
   1 tsp. vanilla
   ¼ tsp. salt
Press Filling evenly over
cookie mixture in pan

CRUMBLE and sprinkle over
top of Filling
   Reserved 1 c. of dough

BAKE at: 350°F.

TIME: 25 min.

Cool

Cut in 1½″ x 1″ bars

YIELD: 54 bars

BUTTERSCOTCH TOFFEE TOPPERS

Preheat oven to 375°F.

COMBINE and mix till crumbly
   1½ c. sifted flour
   ¾ c. firmly packed
      brown sugar
   ½ c. soft butter
   ¼ tsp. salt
Press into 13″ x 9″ x 2″ pan

BAKE at: 375°F.

TIME: 10 min.

TOPPING

COMBINE and stir over hot
(not boiling) water till smooth
   1 6-oz. pkg. (1 c.) Nestlé's
      Butterscotch Morsels
   ¼ c. corn syrup
   2 tbs. shortening
   1 tbs. water
   ¼ tsp. salt
Remove from water

ADD and stir till blended
   2 c. coarsely chopped nuts

SPOON over top of baked cookie
mixture and spread evenly
   Butterscotch Topping

BAKE at: 375°F.

TIME: 8 min.

Cut into bars while warm

YIELD: 2 dozen bars

BUTTERSCOTCH RAISIN BARS
Preheat oven to 375°F.

COOKIE MIXTURE
SIFT together and set aside
  1¾ c. sifted flour
  1 tsp. baking soda
  1 tsp. salt

COMBINE and beat till creamy
  1 c. sugar
  ½ c. butter or shortening
  1 tsp. vanilla

BEAT in, one at a time
  2 eggs

STIR in gradually; mix well
  Flour mixture
Spread in greased
15" x 10" x 1" pan

TOPPING
COMBINE and bring to boil over moderate heat, stirring constantly
  ¼ c. light corn syrup
  2 tbs. water
Remove from heat

ADD and stir till melted
  1 6-oz. pkg. (1 c.)
    Butterscotch Morsels

STIR in
  ½ c. raisins
  ½ c. coarsely chopped nuts
Spread Topping evenly over top of Cookie Mixture. Run knife through mixture to marbleize

BAKE at: 375°F.
TIME: 20 to 25 min.
Spread while warm with

GLAZE
COMBINE and stir till smooth
  2½ c. sifted
    confectioners' sugar
  ⅓ c. orange juice
  1 tsp. grated orange rind
Cool. Cut in 3" x 1" bars
YIELD: 50 bars

BUTTERSCOTCH SCOTCHIES
Preheat oven to 350°F.

MELT over hot (not boiling) water
  1 6-oz. pkg. (1 c.)
    Butterscotch Morsels
  ¼ c. butter or shortening
Remove from heat

STIR in till blended
  1 c. firmly packed brown sugar
Cool approx. 5 min.

STIR in
  2 eggs
  ½ tsp. vanilla

SIFT together and stir in
  ¾ c. sifted flour
  1 tsp. baking powder
  ¾ tsp. salt

STIR in
  ½ c. coarsely chopped nuts
Spread in greased
13" x 9" x 2" pan

BAKE at: 350°F.
TIME: 25 min.
Cut into bars or squares while warm
YIELD: 2 dozen 2" squares

BUTTERSCOTCH NUT SQUARES

Preheat oven to 350°F.

MELT over hot (not boiling) water
   1 6-oz. pkg. (1 c.)
     Butterscotch Morsels
Remove from water

SIFT together and set aside
   ½ c. sifted flour
   ½ tsp. salt
   ¼ tsp. baking powder

COMBINE and beat well
   ½ c. firmly packed brown sugar
   ¼ c. vegetable shortening
   2 eggs
   ½ tsp. vanilla

ADD and mix well
   Melted butterscotch
   ½ c. coarsely chopped nuts
   Sifted flour
Spread in greased 9″ square pan

COMBINE and sprinkle over batter
   ½ c. coarsely chopped nuts
   1 tbs. butter, melted
   1 tbs. sugar

BAKE at: 350°F.

TIME: 25 min.

Cut in squares while warm
Cool in pan

       YIELD: 16 squares
(See illustration 12)

OCTOBER CALICO SQUARES

TOPPING

COMBINE and stir to blend
   1 c. slivered almonds
   ½ c. chopped, candied cherries
   ½ c. raisins
   2 slightly beaten eggs
   1 tbs. sugar
   1 tbs. grated orange rind
Set aside

Preheat oven to 350°F.

COOKIE MIXTURE

SIFT together and set aside
   1⅓ c. sifted flour
   ½ tsp. baking soda
   ⅛ tsp. salt

MELT over hot (not boiling) water
   1 6-oz. pkg. (1 c.)
     Butterscotch Morsels
   ½ c. shortening
Remove from heat

BEAT in gradually
   ½ c. firmly packed brown sugar

STIR in
   Flour mixture
Spread in greased 13″ x 9″ x 2″ pan

BAKE at: 350°F.

TIME: 15 min.

Remove from oven

COVER evenly with
   Topping
Return to oven

BAKE at: 350°F.

TIME: 20 min.

Cool
Cut in 2″ squares*

      YIELD: approx. 2 dozen
*Or cut in 2″ x 1″ bars

      YIELD: approx. 4 dozen

COFFEE-TOFFEE BARS

Preheat oven to 350°F.

SIFT together and set aside
- 2¼ c. sifted flour
- ½ tsp. baking powder
- ¼ tsp. salt

BLEND
- 1 c. butter
- 1 c. firmly packed brown sugar
- 1 tsp. Nescafé
- 1 tsp. almond extract

BLEND in gradually
Dry ingredients

STIR in
- 1 6-oz. pkg. (1 c.) Semi-Sweet Chocolate Morsels
- ½ c. chopped nuts

Press dough into greased 15" x 10" x 1" pan

BAKE at: 350°F.

TIME: 20 to 25 min.

Cut into squares while warm

YIELD: approx. 3 dozen

SANDWICH CRUNCH BARS

Preheat oven to 350°F.

SIFT together and set aside
- 1¼ c. sifted flour
- ¼ tsp. salt

COMBINE and beat till creamy
- ⅓ c. firmly packed brown sugar
- ⅓ c. soft butter

BLEND in
Flour mixture*

Press into a 13" x 9" x 2" pan

BAKE at: 350°F.

TIME: 14 to 16 min.

SPREAD over top at once
¾ c. chunk-style peanut butter

Let stand till cool

TOPPING

PLACE over hot (not boiling) water till butterscotch melts
- 1 6-oz. pkg. (1 c.) Butterscotch Morsels
- 2 tbs. corn syrup
- 1 tbs. water

Stir till blended and smooth

ADD and mix well
2 c. corn flakes

Spread over peanut butter and let stand till set

Cut in 2" x 1" bars

YIELD: 48 bars

*Mixture will be crumbly at this point

page 48 / cookies

CANDY BAR COOKIES

Preheat oven to 325°F.

SIFT and set aside
2 c. sifted flour
¼ tsp. salt

COMBINE and beat till creamy
¾ c. butter
¾ c. sifted confectioners' sugar

ADD and mix well
2 tbs. evaporated milk
1 tsp. vanilla

BLEND in
Sifted flour

Roll out dough, half at a time, to ⅛″ thickness. Cut into 3″ x 1½″ rectangles or 2″ squares; place on ungreased cookie sheets

BAKE at: 325°F.

TIME: 12 to 15 min. or till lightly browned
Cool

YIELD: approx. 3 dozen

Prepare

FILLING

COMBINE in top of double boiler
28 (½ lb.) light colored candy caramels
¼ c. evaporated milk

Heat over boiling water until caramels melt, stirring occasionally

Remove from heat

ADD and mix thoroughly
1 c. sifted confectioners' sugar
¼ c. butter

STIR in
1 c. pecans, chopped

Keep mixture warm over hot water
Spread 1 to 2 tsp. Filling on each cookie

Prepare

ICING

COMBINE and melt over low heat
1 6-oz. pkg. (1 c.) Semi-Sweet Chocolate Morsels
¼ c. evaporated milk

Remove from heat

ADD and mix thoroughly
2 tbs. butter
1 tsp. vanilla
½ c. sifted confectioners' sugar

Top each cookie with ½ tsp. Icing

CHEWY HONEY STICKS

Preheat oven to 400°F.

SIFT together and set aside
1½ c. sifted flour
1 tsp. baking powder
½ tsp. salt

COMBINE and beat till creamy
½ c. shortening
¼ c. sugar
1 tsp. cinnamon
1 tsp. vanilla

BEAT in
1 egg

ADD
¾ c. honey
alternately with
Flour mixture

ADD
1 6-oz. pkg. (1 c.) Semi-Sweet Chocolate Morsels

Spread in greased 15″ x 10″ x 1″ pan

BAKE at: 400°F.

TIME: 12 min.

Cool

Dust with sifted confectioners' sugar, if desired

Cut in 3″ x 1″ sticks

YIELD: approx. 4 dozen

DOUBLE-SCOTCH PECAN BARS

Preheat oven to 350°F.

SIFT together and set aside
- 2 c. sifted flour
- ¾ tsp. salt
- ½ tsp. baking powder

STIR to soften
- ¾ c. butter or margarine

BLEND in
- 1 c. firmly packed brown sugar

BEAT in
- 1 egg
- ½ tsp. vanilla

ADD and stir to blend after each addition
- Flour mixture alternately with
- ¼ c. milk

FOLD in
- 1 6-oz. pkg. (1 c.) Butterscotch Morsels
- 1 c. flaked coconut
- 1 c. chopped pecans

Spread evenly in greased 13" x 9" x 2" pan

BAKE at: 350°F.

TIME: 25 to 30 min.

Cool

Prepare

BUTTERSCOTCH TOPPING

MELT over hot (not boiling) water
- 1 6-oz. pkg. (1 c.) Butterscotch Morsels
- 1 tsp. salad or cooking oil

ADD and stir vigorously till smooth and blended
- 2 tbs. water

Spread on cooled baked mixture

Cut in 2" x 1" bars

YIELD: 4 dozen bars

QUICK PARTY BARS

Preheat oven to 350°F.

COMBINE and beat till creamy
- ½ c. soft butter
- ½ c. firmly packed brown sugar
- 1 tsp. vanilla

BEAT in
- 1 egg

ADD
- ½ c. sifted flour
- ½ c. rolled oats

Spread in greased 11" x 7" x 1½" pan

BAKE at: 350°F.

TIME: 20 min.

Cool slightly

COMBINE and melt over hot (not boiling) water
- 1 6-oz. pkg. (1 c.) Semi-Sweet Chocolate Morsels
- 1 tsp. shortening

Spread over baked mixture

SPRINKLE with
- ½ c. finely chopped nuts

Cut in 3½" x 1¼" bars

YIELD: 16 bars

PETITS FOUR SQUARES

Preheat oven to 350°F.

SIFT together and set aside
  2 c. sifted flour
  ½ tsp. baking powder
  ⅛ tsp. salt

COMBINE and beat till creamy
  1 c. butter
  2 tsp. vanilla
  1 c. firmly packed brown sugar

ADD and blend well
  Flour mixture
  1¾ 6-oz. pkgs. (1¾ c.)
    Semi-Sweet Chocolate Morsels
  ½ c. toasted almonds,
    finely chopped

Spread evenly in an ungreased
13″ x 9″ x 2″ pan

BAKE at: 350°F.

TIME: 30 min.

Cool

FROSTING

COMBINE
  1½ c. sifted confectioners' sugar
  2 tbs. light corn syrup
  1 tbs. milk
  ¼ tsp. vanilla
Spread on cooled baked cookie
Decorate with

GLAZE

MELT over hot (not boiling) water
  ¼ 6-oz. pkg. (¼ c.)
    Semi-Sweet Chocolate Morsels
  1½ tsp. vegetable shortening
Drizzle* in thin lines, lengthwise,
about 1″ apart over Frosting

Using tip of knife or toothpick,
mark crosswise through lines of
Glaze, starting down from one side
of pan and up from opposite side.
Continue marking in alternate directions to give a "feathered" look

Let stand till frosting is set

Cut in 1″ squares

YIELD: 8 doz.

*Or apply with pastry tube, using
small round opening

CRISPIE FUDGE BARS

Preheat oven to 350°F.

MELT over hot (not boiling) water
  1 6-oz. pkg. (1 c.) Semi-Sweet
    Chocolate Morsels
Remove from water

SIFT together and set aside
  1½ c. sifted flour
  1 tsp. baking powder
  ½ tsp. salt

COMBINE and beat till creamy
  ½ c. soft butter
  1 tsp. vanilla

BEAT in gradually
  ¾ c. firmly packed brown sugar

ADD gradually
  Flour mixture

STIR in
  1½ c. finely chopped nuts
  Melted semi-sweet

Spread in 13″ x 9″ x 2″ pan

BAKE at: 350°F.

TIME: approx. 18 to 20 min.

Cut in 2″ x 1″ bars while warm

Cool

YIELD: approx. 4 dozen

THREE-TONE PARTY SQUARES
Preheat oven to 375°F.

SIFT together and set aside
 1¼ c. sifted flour
 ¼ tsp. salt

COMBINE and beat till light
 ⅓ c. firmly packed brown sugar
 ⅓ c. soft butter

BLEND in
 Flour mixture

Press firmly into a 9″ square pan

BAKE at: 375°F.
TIME: 10 min.

TOPPING
COMBINE and beat till thick and lemon colored
 ¾ c. firmly packed brown sugar
 2 eggs
 ¼ tsp. salt

FOLD in gradually
 1½ c. ground walnuts
 1 tsp. vanilla

Spread evenly over baked layer in pan

BAKE at: 375°F.
TIME: approx. 15 min.

Cool in pan
Prepare

GLAZE
MELT over hot (not boiling) water
 1 6-oz. pkg. (1 c.) Semi-Sweet Chocolate Morsels

Remove from water

STIR in
 ½ c. coarsely chopped walnuts
 2 tbs. corn syrup
 1½ tsp. water

Spread on baked mixture
Let stand till Topping is firm
Cut in 1½″ squares

YIELD: 3 dozen

CHOCOLATE SUGAR-PECAN BARS
Preheat oven to 325°F.

TOPPING
COMBINE and set aside
 1 c. pecans, finely chopped
 ½ c. sugar
 2 tsp. hot water
 ¼ tsp. salt

COOKIE MIXTURE
COMBINE and melt over hot (not boiling) water
 2 6-oz. pkgs. or 1 12-oz. pkg. (2 c.) Semi-Sweet Chocolate Morsels
 ½ c. butter

Remove from water

BLEND in
 ¼ c. sugar

BEAT in, one at a time
 2 eggs

STIR in gradually
 2 c. sifted flour

Spread evenly in ungreased 15″ x 10″ x 1″ pan

SPRINKLE over
 Topping

BAKE at: 325°F.
TIME: 20 min.

Cool. Cut in 2″ x 1″ bars

YIELD: approx. 6 dozen

page 52 / cookies

Real Cool Refrigerator Cookies

What a blessing to have this kind of company-insurance! You put these cookies together at your leisure, roll and store them in the refrigerator until they are needed.

CHOCOLATE REFRIGERATOR COOKIES

MELT over hot (not boiling) water
  2 6-oz. pkgs. or 1 12-oz. pkg.
    (2 c.) Semi-Sweet
    Chocolate Morsels
SIFT together and set aside
  3 c. sifted flour
  3 tsp. baking powder
  2 tsp. salt

COMBINE and beat till creamy
  ½ c. shortening
  3 tsp. vanilla
BEAT in gradually
  1 c. firmly packed brown sugar
BEAT in one at a time
  2 eggs
ADD and mix well
  Flour mixture
  Melted semi-sweet
  1 c. nuts, finely chopped
Shape on waxed paper in three 10″ rolls. Roll up. Chill several hours or overnight
Preheat oven to 375°F.
Unroll. Cut in ⅛″ slices. Place on ungreased cookie sheet
BAKE at: 375°F.
TIME: 6 to 8 min.
            YIELD: approx. 20 dozen

CHOC-OAT CRISPS

MELT over hot (not boiling) water
  1 6-oz. pkg. (1 c.) Semi-Sweet
    Chocolate Morsels
Remove from water
SIFT together and set aside
  2 c. sifted flour
  1 tsp. baking powder
  ½ tsp. salt
COMBINE in bowl and beat till light and creamy
  1 c. soft butter
  1 c. sugar
  1 egg
  3 tsp. vanilla
ADD and stir till blended
  Flour mixture
  Melted semi-sweet
  1 c. rolled oats, uncooked
            (continued on page 53)

(continued from page 52)
Chill till firm enough to handle
Shape on waxed paper in two 12″ rolls
Wrap tightly in waxed paper and chill several hours or overnight
Preheat oven to 375°F.
Cut in ¼″ slices and place on ungreased cookie sheets, 1″ apart
BAKE at: 375°F.
TIME: 10 to 12 min.
              YIELD: 8 dozen

JUMBO BARS

SIFT together and set aside
   3½ c. sifted flour
   1 tsp. baking soda
   1 tsp. cinnamon
   ½ tsp. nutmeg
   ½ tsp. salt
COMBINE and beat till creamy
   ⅔ c. butter
   3 tsp. vanilla
BLEND in gradually
   1 c. firmly packed brown sugar
   1 c. granulated sugar
BEAT in
   1 egg
STIR in
   Flour mixture
      alternately with
   ½ c. sour cream
ADD and mix well
   1½ 6-oz. pkgs. (1½ c.) Semi-Sweet Chocolate Morsels
   1½ c. raisins
   ½ c. finely chopped nuts
Spread mixture in 15″ x 10″ x 1″ pan*, lined with waxed paper
Chill for several hours or overnight
Preheat oven to 400°F.
Invert pan on wooden board. Remove cookie mixture and peel off waxed paper
Cut in 2″ x 1½″ bars
Place on ungreased cookie sheet 2″ apart
BAKE at: 400°F.
TIME: 12 min.
              YIELD: 50 bars
*Or make "pan", 15″ x 10″ x 1″, with heavy-duty aluminum foil
(See illustration 22)

CHOCOLATE-NUT MOSAICS
FILLING

MELT over hot (not boiling) water
 1 6-oz. pkg. (1 c.) Semi-Sweet
  Chocolate Morsels
 1 tbs. shortening
Remove from heat

ADD and mix well
 1 c. finely chopped walnuts

BLEND in thoroughly
 1/3 c. sweetened condensed milk
 1 tsp. vanilla
 1/4 tsp. salt

Cool till firm. Turn out on waxed paper and shape into roll 12″ long. Wrap and chill

COOKIE DOUGH

SIFT together and set aside
 1 c. sifted flour
 3/4 tsp. salt
 1/4 tsp. baking powder

BLEND till creamy
 1/2 c. firmly packed brown sugar
 1/4 c. soft butter

BEAT in
 1 egg yolk
 1/2 tsp. vanilla

ADD and mix well
 Flour mixture

Press into firm ball and roll out on waxed paper to rectangle 12″ x 9″

UNWRAP
 Filling

PLACE along 12″ edge of
  Rolled Cookie Dough

Roll up to cover Filling

Wrap in waxed paper and chill till firm

Preheat oven to 375°F.

Unwrap and cut in 1/2″ slices. Place on ungreased cookie sheet

BAKE at: 375°F.

TIME: approx. 10 min.

YIELD: 2 dozen
(See illustration 9)

BON BON TEA CAKES

Preheat oven to 350°F.

SIFT together and set aside
 2 1/2 c. sifted flour
 3/4 tsp. salt

COMBINE in bowl and beat till creamy
 1 c. soft butter
 3/4 c. firmly packed brown sugar
 1 tsp. vanilla

ADD gradually
 Flour mixture

STIR in
 2 c. chopped nuts
 1 6-oz. pkg. (1 c.) Semi-Sweet
  Chocolate Morsels

Form into 1″ balls

Place on ungreased cookie sheet

BAKE at: 350°F.

TIME: 15 min.

While still warm, roll in granulated or sifted confectioners' sugar, if desired. Cool and roll again in sugar, if necessary

YIELD: approx. 6 dozen

CHOCOLATE FROSTEDS

Preheat oven to 350°F.

SIFT together into large bowl
- 1¾ c. sifted flour
- 2 tsp. baking powder
- 1 tsp. salt

ADD and beat till smooth and light
- 1 c. firmly packed brown sugar
- ½ c. soft butter
- 2 eggs
- ⅓ c. milk
- 1 tsp. vanilla

STIR in
- 1½ 6-oz. pkgs. (1½ c.) Semi-Sweet Chocolate Morsels
- 1 c. chopped walnuts

Drop by slightly rounded teaspoonfuls 2″ apart onto greased cookie sheet

BAKE at: 350°F.

TIME: 12 min.

Cool

Prepare

FROSTING

MELT over hot (not boiling) water
- ½ 6-oz. pkg. (½ c.) Semi-Sweet Chocolate Morsels

Remove from heat

STIR in and set aside
- ⅓ c. hot water
- ½ tsp. Nescafé

COMBINE and beat till fluffy
- 1 c. sifted confectioners' sugar
- ⅓ c. soft butter
- ½ tsp. vanilla
- ⅛ tsp. salt

ADD, mixing well after each addition
- 3 c. sifted confectioners' sugar alternately with
- Semi-sweet mixture

Frost cooled cookies

YIELD: approx. 3 dozen

HARLEQUIN DIPPERS

Preheat oven to 325°F.

COMBINE and beat till light and fluffy
- 1 c. soft butter
- 1 c. sifted confectioners' sugar

ADD
- 2 c. sifted flour
- 1 c. rolled oats
- 2 tsp. vanilla
- ¾ tsp. salt

Shape into 1″ balls, or shape into 1½″ logs

Place on ungreased cookie sheet

PRESS into center, if desired
- Walnut half

BAKE at: 325°F.

TIME: 25 min.

Cool

Prepare

CHOCOLATE GLAZE

MELT over hot (not boiling) water
- 1 6-oz. pkg. (1 c.) Semi-Sweet Chocolate Morsels
- 1 tsp. shortening

Remove from heat

DIP top or ends of each cookie into Chocolate Glaze

DIP into
- Finely chopped walnuts

YIELD: approx. 5 dozen

BUTTERSCOTCH THINS

MELT over hot (not boiling) water
    1 6-oz. pkg. (1 c.)
        Butterscotch Morsels
    ½ c. butter or margarine
Remove from heat

ADD and beat till light-colored
    ⅔ c. firmly packed brown sugar
    1 egg

SIFT together and stir into
butterscotch mixture
    1⅓ c. sifted flour
    ¾ tsp. baking soda

ADD
    ⅓ c. chopped nuts
    ¾ tsp. vanilla

Chill till firm enough to handle

Shape on waxed paper in one 12″
roll. Roll up and chill thoroughly*

Preheat oven to 375°F.

Cut in very thin slices

Place on ungreased cookie sheet

BAKE at: 375°F.

TIME: 5 to 6 min.

Let cool approx. 1 min., then
remove from pan

        YIELD: approx. 8 dozen

*Or wrap in foil and freeze
(See illustration 9)

DATE BUTTERSCOTCH COOKIES

SIFT together and set aside
    3½ c. sifted flour
    1 tsp. soda
    1 tsp. cream of tartar
    ½ tsp. salt

MELT over hot (not boiling) water
    1 6-oz. pkg. (1 c.)
        Butterscotch Morsels
Remove from water

BLEND till light
    1½ c. firmly packed brown sugar
    ⅔ c. vegetable shortening

BEAT in, one at a time
    3 eggs

STIR in
    Melted butterscotch
    1 tsp. vanilla

ADD and stir to blend
    Flour mixture
        alternately with
    2 tbs. water

Chill till firm enough to handle

Shape in two 12″ rolls. Wrap in
waxed paper. Chill thoroughly

Preheat oven to 350°F.

FILLING

COMBINE in saucepan and cook till
thick
    1 8-oz. pkg. dates,
    chopped (1¼ c.)
    ½ c. firmly packed brown sugar
    ½ c. water

STIR in
    ½ c. finely chopped nuts

Cool

Cut chilled cookie roll in ⅛″ slices.
Arrange half the slices on greased
cookie sheet

PLACE on each slice
    ½ tsp. Filling

Top with remaining slices. Press
edges together with tines of fork

BAKE at: 350°F.

TIME: 10 min.

        YIELD: 7 dozen

Happy Holiday Cookies

BEAU CATCHERS
CHOCOLATE DATE FILLING

MELT over hot (not boiling) water
  1 6-oz. pkg. (1 c.) Semi-Sweet Chocolate Morsels
Remove from heat

ADD and stir till blended
  ¾ c. marshmallow cream
  ¼ c. sifted confectioners' sugar
  2 tsp. water
  ⅛ tsp. salt

STIR in
  1 c. finely chopped dates
  ¼ c. chopped nuts
  1 tbs. grated orange rind

Cool

Shape into 1¼" balls using one well-rounded teaspoon for each

Chill

Prepare

COOKIE MIXTURE

SIFT together and set aside
  2 c. sifted flour
  ½ tsp. baking soda
  ½ tsp. salt

COMBINE and place over hot (not boiling) water till chocolate melts
  1 6-oz. pkg. (1 c.) Semi-Sweet Chocolate Morsels
  1 tbs. water
  1 tsp. vanilla

Stir till smooth

Remove from heat

COMBINE and beat till light and creamy
  ½ c. soft shortening
  ½ c. firmly packed brown sugar
  1 egg

STIR in gradually
  Flour mixture

ADD and blend well
  Semi-sweet mixture

Shape one rounded tablespoon of dough around each chilled ball of filling

Seal well

Place on ungreased cookie sheet
Chill about 30 min.

Preheat oven to 400°F.

BAKE at: 400°F.

TIME: 6 min.

Cool thoroughly before removing from cookie sheet

YIELD: 2 dozen
(continued on page 58)

page 58 | cookies

(continued from page 57)

Variations:

1. MACAROON FILLING:

COMBINE and beat till soft peaks form
  1 egg white
  1 tbs. vanilla
  ⅛ tsp. salt

ADD gradually and beat till stiff and glossy
  ¼ c. sugar

STIR in
  1 7-oz. pkg. (2 c.)
    grated coconut
Shape into 1″ balls, using one well-rounded teaspoon for each
Chill

2. BUTTERSCOTCH CRISPY FILLING:

MELT over hot (not boiling) water
  ½ 6-oz. pkg. (½ c.)
    Butterscotch Morsels

STIR in
  1 c. marshmallow cream
  ½ tsp. vanilla

PLACE in bowl
  1½ c. oven-toasted rice cereal

ADD and stir till well blended
  Butterscotch mixture
Shape into 1″ balls, using one well-rounded teaspoon for each
Chill

3. COFFEE FILLING:

COMBINE and mix well
  1 tbs. Nescafé
  1 tbs. water

ADD and stir till well blended
  1 c. finely chopped nuts
  1 c. vanilla wafer crumbs
    (35 small wafers)
  ½ c. marshmallow cream

  ¼ c. brown sugar
  ¼ tsp. salt
Shape into 1¼″ balls, using one well-rounded teaspoon for each
Chill

FESTIVE CLUSTERS
Preheat oven to 325°F.

SIFT together and set aside
  ¾ c. sifted flour
  ¾ tsp. baking soda
  ¾ tsp. cinnamon
  ½ tsp. salt
  ¼ tsp. cloves
  ¼ tsp. nutmeg

COMBINE and beat till light
  ¼ c. firmly packed brown sugar
  1 egg
  2 tsp. rum extract

BLEND in
  2 tbs. butter, melted

STIR in gradually
  Flour mixture
    alternately with
  ¼ c. milk

ADD and stir till well coated
  2 6-oz. pkgs. or 1 12-oz. pkg.
    (2 c.) Semi-Sweet
    Chocolate Morsels
  2 c. pecan halves
  1 3½-oz. pkg. (1⅓ c.)
    flaked coconut
  1 c. candied cherries
  ½ c. diced, preserved citron

Drop on greased cookie sheet, using 1 heaping tsp. for each

BAKE at: 325°F.

TIME: approx. 15 min.

Remove from pan immediately

  YIELD: approx. 7 dozen
  (See illustration 26)

FLORENTINE DAINTIES

Preheat oven to 325°F.

SIFT together and set aside
- ½ c. sifted flour
- ¼ tsp. salt

COMBINE and beat till very thick and lemon colored
- 2 eggs
- ½ c. sugar

FOLD in
- Flour mixture

STIR in
- 1 6-oz. pkg. (1 c.) Semi-Sweet Chocolate Morsels
- ¾ c. chopped dates
- ¾ c. chopped walnuts
- 1 tbs. grated lemon rind

Drop by rounded teaspoonfuls, 2″ apart, on cookie sheet lined with well-greased foil

BAKE at: 325°F.

TIME: 12 to 15 min.

Remove immediately from cookie sheet

Cool

Decorate with

GLAZE

MELT over hot (not boiling) water and stir till blended
- 1 6-oz. pkg. (1 c.) Semi-Sweet Chocolate Morsels
- 1 tbs. shortening

Drizzle over cookies in crisscross lines

YIELD: approx. 6 dozen

When semi-sweet sets, store in tightly covered container in layers, with foil between each layer

page 60 / cookies

PEEKABOO BON BONS
COOKIE MIXTURE

COMBINE and beat till creamy
  1 c. soft butter
  1 c. sifted confectioners' sugar

ADD gradually, blending well after each addition
  2 c. sifted flour
  2 tsp. vanilla
  ¾ tsp. salt

Chill till firm enough to handle

Shape into balls, using a well-rounded teaspoon of dough for each

Chill till Filling is prepared

CHOCOLATE FILLING

MELT over hot (not boiling) water
  1 6-oz. pkg. (1 c.) Semi-Sweet Chocolate Morsels
  1 tsp. shortening
Remove from water

ADD and stir to blend
  1 c. finely chopped walnuts
  ⅓ c. sweetened condensed milk
  1 tsp. water
  ½ tsp. vanilla

Shape into balls, using a *level* teaspoon of Filling for each

Preheat oven to 350°F.

To combine: Flatten ball of Cookie Mixture and place ball of Filling in center. Bring Cookie Mixture up around Filling, leaving a little of the Filling showing

Roll quickly into ball again*

Continue like this with remaining Cookie Mixture and Filling

Place on ungreased cookie sheet

BAKE at: 350°F.

TIME: 12 to 14 min.

  YIELD: approx. 5 dozen

*If desired, roll in finely chopped walnuts

(See illustration 8)

CHOCOLATE CRACKLERS

Preheat oven to 375°F.

SIFT together and set aside
  1 c. sifted flour
  1 tsp. salt
  ½ tsp. baking powder

MELT over hot (not boiling) water
  1 6-oz. pkg. (1 c.) Semi-Sweet Chocolate Morsels

Remove from water

Cool

COMBINE and beat till light and creamy
  1 c. sugar
  ½ c. soft butter
  1½ tsp. vanilla

BEAT in
  2 eggs

BLEND in
  Melted semi-sweet

ADD and mix well
  Flour mixture

STIR in
  1½ c. chopped nuts

Drop by rounded tablespoonfuls on ungreased cookie sheets. Place whole walnut half on each, if desired

BAKE at: 375°F.

TIME: 10 min.

  YIELD: approx. 2 dozen

(See illustration 22)

POLKA DOT PLATTERS

Preheat oven to 375°F.

SIFT together and set aside
- 2 c. sifted flour
- 2 tsp. baking powder
- 1 tsp. salt
- ¾ tsp. baking soda

COMBINE and beat till light and creamy
- 2 c. firmly packed brown sugar
- 1 c. soft butter

BEAT in
- 2 eggs

STIR in
- 1 tbs. water
- 1½ tsp. grated orange rind

ADD and mix well
- Flour mixture

STIR in
- 1½ c. rolled oats
- 1 6-oz. pkg. (1 c.) Semi-Sweet Chocolate Morsels
- ½ c. chopped walnuts

Drop by rounded tablespoonfuls, 3″ apart, on lightly greased cookie sheets

BAKE at: 375°F.

TIME: approx. 12 min.

YIELD: 3 dozen

MINCEMEAT JUMBLES

Preheat oven to 375°F.

SIFT together and set aside
- 2½ c. sifted flour
- 2 tsp. baking soda
- 1 tsp. salt.

COMBINE and beat till creamy
- 1 c. sugar
- ½ c. shortening

BEAT in, one at a time
- 3 eggs

Continue beating till light

STIR in
- Flour mixture
- 2 6-oz. pkgs. or 1 12-oz. pkg. (2 c.) Semi-Sweet Chocolate Morsels
- 1¾ c. (1-lb. 2½-oz. jar) mincemeat

Drop by tablespoonfuls on a greased and floured cookie sheet

BAKE at: 375°F.

TIME: 10 min.

YIELD: 4 dozen

page 61 / cookies

CHOCOLATE-OAT SUGAR BALLS

Preheat oven to 375°F.

SIFT together and set aside
 1¼ c. sifted flour
 ½ tsp. baking soda
 ½ tsp. salt

MELT over hot (not boiling) water
 1 6-oz. pkg. (1 c.) Semi-Sweet
  Chocolate Morsels
 ½ c. shortening

Remove from heat

ADD and beat thoroughly
 ½ c. firmly packed brown sugar
 1 egg
 1 tsp. vanilla

STIR in
 Flour mixture
 1 c. rolled oats

Shape into balls, using 1 level teaspoon for each, and place on greased cookie sheet

BAKE at: 375°F.

TIME: 6 to 8 min.

Roll in sugar while still warm

YIELD: approx. 7 dozen

CHOCOLATE PEPPERMINT CREAMS

Preheat oven to 350°F.

SIFT together and set aside
 3 c. sifted flour
 1¼ tsp. baking soda
 1 tsp. salt

COMBINE in saucepan and stir constantly over moderate heat till butter is melted
 1½ c. firmly packed brown sugar
 ¾ c. butter

Remove from heat

STIR in
 2 tbs. water

ADD and stir till semi-sweet melts, and mixture is smooth
 2 6-oz. pkgs. or 1 12-oz. pkg.
  (2 c.) Semi-Sweet
  Chocolate Morsels

BEAT in
 2 eggs

ADD gradually, mixing well after each addition
 Flour mixture

Drop by heaping teaspoonfuls onto greased cookie sheet

BAKE at: 350°F.

TIME: 8 to 10 min.

Cool

Prepare

PEPPERMINT CREAM

COMBINE and beat till light and fluffy
 1 c. sifted confectioners' sugar
 ⅓ c. soft butter
 ⅛ tsp. salt
 ⅛ tsp. peppermint extract

BLEND in
 2 c. sifted confectioners' sugar
  alternately with
 ¼ c. milk or light cream

SANDWICH each pair of cookies together with
 1 rounded tsp. Peppermint Cream

YIELD: approx. 4 dozen

SAND TARTS
Preheat oven to 350°F.

COMBINE and blend well
- 1 c. soft butter
- 1 tsp. vanilla
- ½ tsp. salt
- ½ tsp. almond extract

BEAT in gradually
- 1¼ c. sugar

BEAT in
- 1 egg

STIR in
- 2 c. sifted flour

ADD
- 1 6-oz. pkg. (1 c.) Semi-Sweet Chocolate Morsels

Drop by teaspoonfuls on ungreased cookie sheet

BAKE at: 350°F.
TIME: 15 min.

YIELD: approx. 6 dozen

CHOCOLATE ALMOND TEAS
Preheat oven to 350°F.

COMBINE and beat till creamy
- ½ c. soft butter
- ¼ c. firmly packed brown sugar
- 2 tbs. water
- 1 tsp. vanilla
- ¼ tsp. salt

ADD and mix well
- 1 c. sifted flour
- ½ c. toasted almonds, finely chopped

ADD
- 1 6-oz. pkg. (1 c.) Semi-Sweet Chocolate Morsels

Drop by rounded teaspoonfuls on ungreased cookie sheet

BAKE at: 350°F.
TIME: 12 min.

ROLL while warm in
- ¾ c. sifted confectioners' sugar

YIELD: approx. 4½ dozen

SANDIES
Preheat oven to 300°F.

COMBINE and blend well
- ¾ c. soft butter
- ⅓ c. sugar
- 1 tbs. water
- 1 tsp. vanilla
- ⅛ tsp. salt

STIR in
- 2 c. sifted flour
- 1 6-oz. pkg. (1 c.) Semi-Sweet Chocolate Morsels

Form in 1″ balls

ROLL in
- 1 c. pecans, finely chopped

Place on ungreased cookie sheet

BAKE at: 300°F.
TIME: 30 min.

Roll in sugar while warm

YIELD: approx. 5 dozen

World-Wide Treasury of Cookies

SWISS FRUIT-NUT COOKIES

Preheat oven to 350°F.

SIFT together and set aside
- ½ c. flour
- ½ tsp. cinnamon
- ½ tsp. salt
- Dash cloves

COMBINE and stir to blend
- 3 eggs
- ½ c. sugar

STIR in
- Flour mixture

ADD
- 1¼ c. finely chopped, blanched almonds
- 1 6-oz. pkg. (1 c.) Semi-Sweet Chocolate Morsels
- ½ c. mixed candied fruit, finely chopped
- ½ tsp. grated lemon rind

Drop by rounded teaspoonfuls onto foil-lined cookie sheet

BAKE at: 350°F.

TIME: 9 min.

Remove immediately

YIELD: approx. 4½ dozen

VIENNESE COOKIES

Preheat oven to 400°F.

COMBINE and beat till creamy
- 1 c. soft butter
- 1 tbs. grated lemon rind
- 1 tsp. salt
- ½ tsp. cinnamon
- ½ tsp. cloves

BEAT in gradually
- 1 c. firmly packed brown sugar

ADD, one at a time, beating till light after each
- 3 eggs

STIR in gradually
- 2 c. sifted flour

ADD and mix well
- 1 6-oz. pkg. (1 c.) Semi-Sweet Chocolate Morsels
- 1 c. pecans, finely chopped

Drop by well-rounded teaspoonfuls on ungreased cookie sheet

BAKE at: 400°F.

TIME: 6 to 8 min.

Store in tightly covered container

YIELD: approx. 6 dozen

CHOCOLATE LEBKUCHEN

SIFT together and set aside
- 2¾ c. sifted flour
- 2 tsp. cinnamon
- 1 tsp. cloves
- 1 tsp. cardamom seeds, finely crushed
- 1 tsp. baking soda
- 1 tsp. baking powder

BRING to boil in saucepan over moderate heat
- 1¼ c. sugar
- ¾ c. honey
- 2 tbs. water

Cool

STIR into honey mixture till blended
- 2 6-oz. pkgs. or 1 12-oz. pkg. (2 c.) Semi-Sweet Chocolate Morsels
- 1 c. chopped walnuts
- ½ c. mixed candied fruit, finely chopped
- 2 eggs, well beaten
- ¼ c. orange juice

BLEND in gradually
Flour mixture

Store dough in tightly covered dish, at room temperature, for 3 days, to ripen

Preheat oven to 325°F.

Spread dough in greased 15" x 10" x 1" pan

BAKE at: 325°F.

TIME: 35 to 40 min.

Cool. Wrap in foil, and store till ready to use. (This keeps very well for several weeks, and improves in flavor on storing)

When ready to use, unwrap and dust with sifted confectioners' sugar or top with confectioners' glaze
Cut in 3" x 1" bars

YIELD: 50 bars
(See illustration 26)

SCANDINAVIAN SNAPPERS

Preheat oven to 350°F.

SIFT together and set aside
- 1¾ c. sifted flour
- 2 tsp. baking soda
- 1 tsp. cinnamon
- ¼ tsp. salt

MELT over hot (not boiling) water
- 1 6-oz. pkg. (1 c.) Semi-Sweet Chocolate Morsels

Remove from heat

COMBINE and beat till creamy
- ⅔ c. shortening
- ½ c. sugar
- 1 egg

BLEND in
Melted semi-sweet
- ¼ c. light corn syrup

STIR in gradually
Flour mixture

ADD and mix well
- 1 c. finely chopped walnuts

Shape dough into balls using 1 level tablespoon for each

ROLL balls of dough in
Sugar (approx. ¼ c.)

Place on ungreased cookie sheets

BAKE at: 350°F.

TIME: 15 min.

Let stand a few minutes before removing from pan

YIELD: 3 dozen 3" cookies
(See illustration 22)

ARABIAN DELIGHTS

Preheat oven to 325°F.

SIFT together and set aside
½ c. sifted flour
1 tsp. baking powder
¼ tsp. salt

ADD
1 c. pitted dates, cut in eighths
1 6-oz. pkg. (1 c.) Semi-Sweet
Chocolate Morsels
1 tbs. grated lemon rind

COMBINE and beat till thick
2 eggs
½ c. sugar

FOLD in
Semi-sweet mixture

Drop by teaspoonfuls on well-
greased cookie sheet

BAKE at: 325°F.

TIME: 12 to 15 min.

YIELD: approx. 4 dozen

ORIENTAL BRITTLE "COOKIES"

Preheat oven to 375°F.

BLEND
1 c. butter
2 tsp. Nescafé
1 tsp. salt
1 tsp. vanilla
½ tsp. almond extract

BEAT in gradually
1 c. sugar

ADD and mix well
2 c. sifted flour
1 6-oz. pkg. (1 c.) Semi-Sweet
Chocolate Morsels

Press into ungreased
15″ x 10″ x 1″ pan

SPRINKLE over top
½ c. almonds, finely chopped

BAKE at: 375°F.

TIME: 25 min.

Cool—then break in irregular
pieces

YIELD: approx. 1¾ lbs.
(See illustration 5)

LACY ENGLISH JUMBOS

Preheat oven to 350°F.

COMBINE and melt over hot
(not boiling) water
1 6-oz. pkg. (1 c.) Semi-Sweet
Chocolate Morsels
¾ c. shortening
¾ c. sugar
⅛ tsp. salt
¼ tsp. ginger
Remove from water

STIR in
½ c. light corn syrup
1½ c. sifted flour

Drop by teaspoonfuls, 3″ apart, on
well-greased cookie sheet

BAKE at: 350°F.

TIME: 10 min.

Cool approx. 1 min. Roll at once
—top side out—over handle of
wooden spoon, or use fingers to
form cone. Press to seal edges. If
cookies stick, return to oven for 1
minute. Then proceed as directed

YIELD: approx. 5 dozen
(See illustration 12)

FRENCH CHOCOLATE MERINGUES

Preheat oven to 350°F.

MELT over hot (not boiling) water
- 1 6-oz. pkg. (1 c.) Semi-Sweet Chocolate Morsels

Remove from water

Cool approx. 5 min.

COMBINE and beat till stiff but not dry
- 3 egg whites
- ½ tsp. vanilla

BEAT in gradually till *very* stiff
- 1 c. sugar

FOLD in
- 1 c. finely crushed, salted crackers
- Cooled semi-sweet

Drop by teaspoonfuls on greased cookie sheets

BAKE at: 350°F.

TIME: approx. 10 min.

Remove from pans immediately

YIELD: 4 dozen

(See illustration 12)

SWEDISH DELICACIES

SIFT together and set aside
- 1¾ c. sifted flour
- ½ tsp. salt
- ¾ tsp. ground ammonium carbonate* *or* baking powder

BLEND
- ½ c. butter
- ½ c. shortening
- ½ tsp. vanilla

BEAT in gradually
- 1 c. sugar

ADD
- Flour mixture
- ½ c. almonds, finely chopped
- 1 6-oz. pkg. (1 c.) Semi-Sweet Chocolate Morsels

Shape on waxed paper in two 9" rolls. Roll up. Chill several hours or overnight

Preheat oven to 375°F.

Unroll. Cut in ⅛" slices. Place on ungreased cookie sheet

BAKE at: 375°F.

TIME: 8 to 10 min.

YIELD: approx. 10 dozen

*May be purchased in drug store

page 68 / cookies

IRISH WHIRLIGIGS

MELT over hot (not boiling) water
　1 6-oz. pkg. (1 c.) Semi-Sweet
　　Chocolate Morsels
Remove from water

SIFT together and set aside
　2½ c. sifted flour
　1¼ tsp. baking powder
　½ tsp. salt

COMBINE and beat till creamy
　1 c. soft butter
　1 c. sugar
　1 egg
　1 tbs. vanilla

BLEND in gradually
　Flour mixture
　1 c. quick-cooking rolled oats

REMOVE and reserve
　1 c. of dough
Chill

ADD to remaining dough
　Melted semi-sweet

Chill till firm enough to handle

ROLL out between two sheets of
waxed paper to 18″ x 10″ rectangle
　Chilled semi-sweet dough
Peel off top sheet of waxed paper

ROLL out between two sheets of
waxed paper to 18″ x 8″ rectangle
　Reserved 1 c. of dough
Peel off top sheet of waxed paper

INVERT on
　Rolled semi-sweet dough
Peel off rest of waxed paper
Starting along 18″ edge, roll up,
like jelly roll
Wrap and chill several hours
Preheat oven to 375°F.
Unwrap dough and cut in ¼″ slices

Place 1″ apart on ungreased cookie
sheet
BAKE at: 375°F.
TIME: 8 min.

　　　YIELD: approx. 6 dozen
　　(See illustration 21)

SWISS CHEWS

Preheat oven to 325°F.

MELT over hot (not boiling) water
　1 6-oz. pkg. (1 c.) Semi-Sweet
　　Chocolate Morsels
Remove from water and cool
5 min.

BEAT till thick
　1 egg

BEAT in gradually, till *very* thick
　½ c. firmly packed brown sugar

FOLD in
　Cooled semi-sweet
　½ c. toasted almonds,
　　finely chopped
　1 tsp. vanilla
　¼ tsp. salt

Drop by teaspoonfuls on greased
cookie sheet
BAKE at: 325°F.
TIME: approx. 10 min.

　　　YIELD: approx. 3 dozen

JAMAICA BANANA BARS

Preheat oven to 350°F.

MELT over hot (not boiling) water
  1 6-oz. pkg. (1 c.) Semi-Sweet Chocolate Morsels

SIFT together and set aside
  1 c. sifted flour
  ¾ c. sugar
  ¾ tsp. cinnamon
  1¼ tsp. salt
  ½ tsp. baking powder
  ¼ tsp. baking soda

COMBINE and beat till blended
  1 c. mashed ripe banana
  ¼ c. butter or margarine

BEAT in
  1 egg

ADD and blend well after each addition
  Flour mixture
    alternately with
  2 tbs. milk

STIR in
  Melted semi-sweet
  1 c. chopped nuts

Spread in greased and floured 13" x 9" x 2" pan

BAKE at: 350°F.

TIME: 25 min.

Cool

Frost with

FROSTING

MELT over hot (not boiling) water
  1 6-oz. pkg. (1 c.) Semi-Sweet Chocolate Morsels
  2 tbs. vegetable shortening

Remove from water

STIR in and beat till smooth
  1½ c. sifted confectioners' sugar
  ¼ c. milk
  ⅛ tsp. salt
  ⅛ tsp. vanilla

Spread over cooled baked mixture

Cut in 2" x 1½" bars

YIELD: 32 bars

NEAR EAST DATE-ORANGE BARS

Preheat oven to 350°F.

SIFT together and set aside
    1¼ c. sifted flour
    ¾ tsp. baking soda
    ½ tsp. salt

COMBINE in large saucepan and cook over low heat, stirring, till dates soften
    1 8-oz. pkg. dates, chopped (1¼ c.)
    ¾ c. firmly packed brown sugar
    ½ c. water
    ½ c. butter
    1 tbs. grated orange rind
Remove from heat

STIR in
    1 6-oz. pkg. (1 c.) Semi-Sweet Chocolate Morsels

BEAT in
    2 eggs

ADD and blend well
    Dry ingredients
        alternately with
    1 c. orange juice

STIR in
    1 c. chopped walnuts
Spread in well-greased 15″ x 10″ x 1″ pan

BAKE at: 350°F.

TIME: 25 to 30 min.

Cool
Spread with

GLAZE

BLEND till creamy
    2 tbs. soft butter
    1 tsp. grated orange rind

STIR in gradually
    1½ c. sifted confectioners' sugar
        alternately with
    1½ tbs. milk
Let stand till Glaze is set
Cut into 3″ x 2″ bars

              YIELD: 25 bars
(See illustration 9)

LATIN AMERICAN COOKIES

Preheat oven to 375°F.

SIFT together and set aside
    1½ c. sifted flour
    ½ tsp. salt
    ½ tsp. baking powder
    ½ tsp. baking soda

COMBINE and beat till creamy
    ⅓ c. butter
    ⅓ c. light molasses
    ¼ c. sugar
    ½ tsp. cinnamon
    ¼ tsp. nutmeg
    ⅛ tsp. ginger

ADD
    Flour mixture
        alternately with
    ⅓ c. water

ADD
    1 6-oz. pkg. (1 c.) Semi-Sweet Chocolate Morsels
Drop by teaspoonfuls on greased cookie sheet

BAKE at: 375°F.

TIME: 8 to 10 min.

        YIELD: approx. 3½ dozen

AUSTRALIAN SQUARES

Preheat oven to 375°F.

COMBINE and blend well
- ½ c. butter
- ¼ c. firmly packed brown sugar
- 1 tbs. grated lemon rind
- 1 tsp. vanilla

BEAT in
- 1 egg yolk

ADD
- 1 c. sifted flour
  alternately with
- ¼ c. water

ADD
- 1 6-oz. pkg. (1 c.) Semi-Sweet Chocolate Morsels

BEAT till stiff but not dry
- 1 egg white

BEAT in gradually till stiff and glossy
- ¼ c. firmly packed brown sugar

FOLD into
  Semi-sweet mixture

Pour in waxed paper-lined 8" square pan

BAKE at: 375°F.

TIME: 25 to 30 min.

SPRINKLE over top while warm
- 2 tbs. sifted confectioners' sugar

Cool. Cut in 2" squares

YIELD: 16

HOLLAND SNAPS

Preheat oven to 350°F.

SIFT together and set aside
- 1 c. sifted flour
- ½ tsp. baking soda
- ⅛ tsp. salt

COMBINE and melt over hot (not boiling) water
- 1 6-oz. pkg. (1 c.) Semi-Sweet Chocolate Morsels
- ½ c. butter
- ⅓ c. sugar
- ¼ c. light corn syrup

Remove from water; stir to blend

Cool approx. 5 min.

ADD and beat well
  Flour mixture
- 1 egg
- 1 tsp. vanilla

Drop by half teaspoonfuls on greased cookie sheet

BAKE at: 350°F.

TIME: 10 min.

YIELD: 6 dozen

page 72 / cookies

Quickies for the Crowd

"EASY-TO-MAKE" DELUXE BROWNIES

Preheat oven to 375°F.

MELT over hot (not boiling) water
  1 6-oz. pkg. (1 c.) Semi-Sweet
    Chocolate Morsels

COMBINE and beat till well blended
  ½ 13½-oz. pkg (1 c. firmly
    packed) Nestlé's All Purpose
    Cookie Mix*
  ¼ c. water
  1 egg
  2 tbs. sugar

ADD and beat till blended
  Melted semi-sweet
  ½ c. chopped nuts (optional)

Pour into waxed paper-lined
8″ square pan

BAKE at: 375°F.

TIME: 25 to 30 min.

  YIELD: 16 2″ squares

*Use remaining Cookie Mix to
make DROP COOKIES: Combine ½
pkg. (1 c.) All Purpose Cookie
Mix with 3 tbs. water. Beat to
blend well

BAKE at: 375°F.

TIME: 10 to 12 min.

  YIELD: 2 dozen

"EASY-TO-MAKE" DROP COOKIES

Preheat oven to 375°F.

BREAK into measuring cup
  1 egg

ADD
  Enough water to make ⅓ c.

STIR into
  1 13½-oz. pkg. Nestlé's
    All Purpose Cookie Mix

Beat till well blended

Drop by teaspoonfuls on ungreased
cookie sheet

BAKE at: 375°F.

TIME: 10 to 12 min.

  YIELD: 4 dozen 2″ cookies

Variations:

1. CEREAL CRISPS: Stir in 2 c.
   ready-to-eat cereal flakes.
2. COCONUT COOKIES: Stir in
   1 c. coconut.
3. DATE-NUT COOKIES: Stir in
   1 c. chopped dates and 1 c.
   chopped nuts.
4. OATMEAL COOKIES: Stir in
   1 c. rolled oats, ½ tsp. cinnamon and ½ tsp. ginger
   or allspice.
5. ORANGE COOKIES: Stir in 1 tbs.
   grated orange rind.
6. PEANUT BUTTER COOKIES:
   Stir in ½ c. peanut butter.
7. RAISIN COOKIES: Stir in 1 c.
   raisins.
8. SPICE COOKIES: Stir in 1 tsp.
   cinnamon, ½ tsp. nutmeg
   and ½ tsp. allspice.
9. TOLL HOUSE COOKIES: Stir in
   1 6-oz. pkg. (1 c.) Semi-Sweet
   Chocolate Morsels and ½ c.
   chopped nuts (optional).

8 Good company with milk for between-meal snacks, or while watching the late-late show: *left,* Chocolate Peanut Butter Oat Cookies (p. 84); *center,* Peek-a-Boo Bon Bons (p. 60); *right,* Crinkly Puffs (p. 84).

9 A line-up of goodness: *(from top to bottom)* Crunchy Sandwich Cookies (p. 85), Butterscotch Thins (p. 56), Near-East Date-Orange Bars (p. 70), Chocolate Nut Mosaics (p. 54) and Corn Flake Meringoons (p. 85).

10 On the mobile: Short Cut Fudge (p. 135) takes many shapes—crescents dipped in chopped nuts, a candy-sprinkled cone, a sugar-iced log. Swinging with them—Walnut Chocolettes (p. 141) spiked with silver *dragées,* colored coconut, slivered nuts. In the apothecary jar just under the mobile: *(from top to bottom)* Two-Tone Mallow Bites (p. 146) and Bourbon Balls (p. 144) rolled in sugar or Strawberry Quik. The other jars *(from left to right)* Ribbon Candies (p. 143), Marshmallow Cream Fudge (p. 138) and Walnut Chocolettes.

11 A sampler for any occasion: *(from top to bottom)* Ribbon Candies (p. 143), Walnut Chocolettes (p. 141), Butterscotch Pralines (p. 138), Strawberry and Chocolate Fruit Balls (p. 144) and Bourbon Balls (p. 144).

12 Good things come in threes—and here are three kinds of delicious company cookies: *(from top to bottom)* Lacy English Jumbos (p. 66), Butterscotch Nut Squares (p. 46) and French Chocolate Meringues (p. 67).

13 Toll House Cookies—an American classic. See pages 31 and 32 for our wonderful variations.

14 For after-school snacks, these Fudge Brownies (p. 41) are the tastiest ever. The Strawberry Quik is more than a milk drink — it's a pink delight you'll want to enjoy again and again.

8

9

10

11

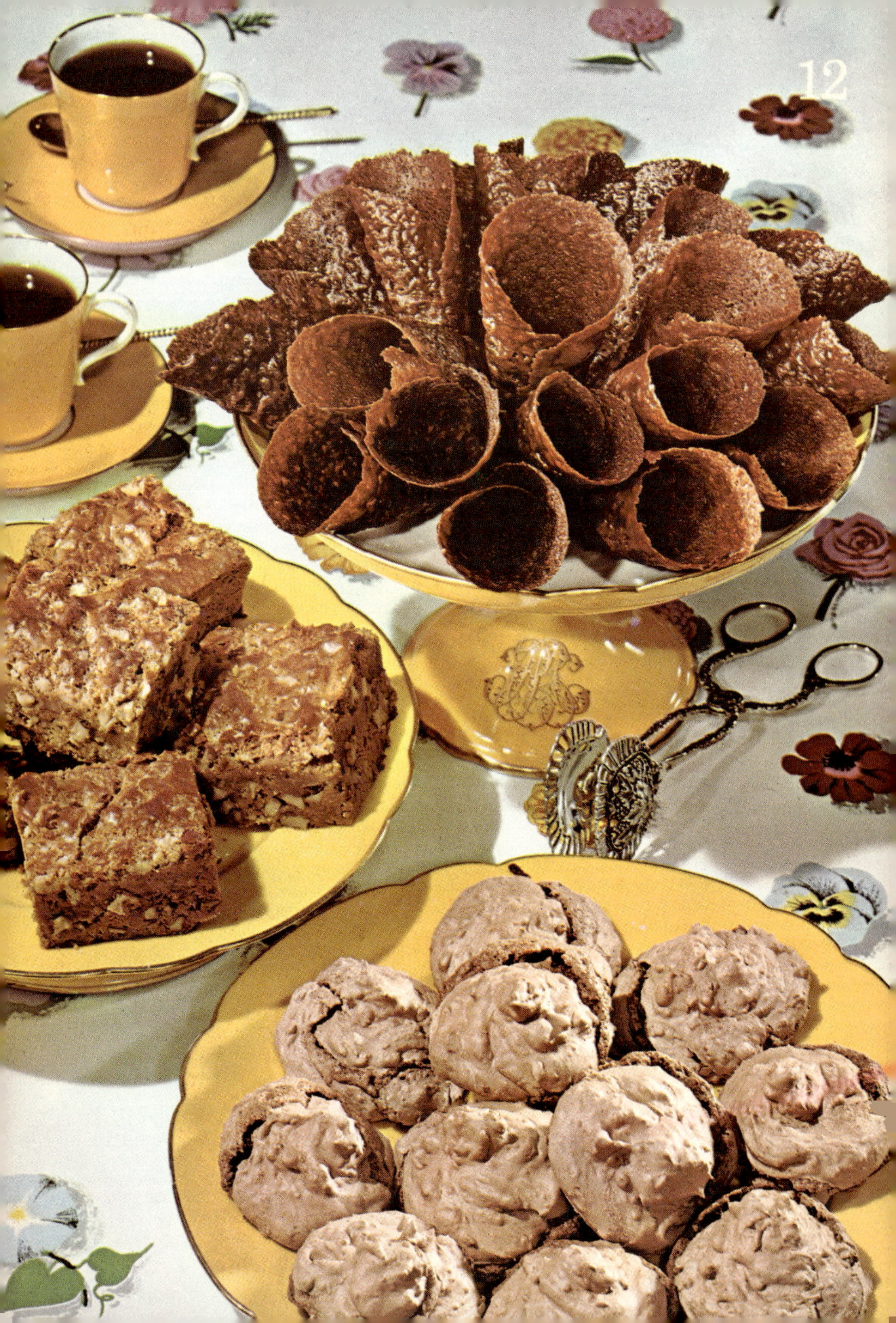
12

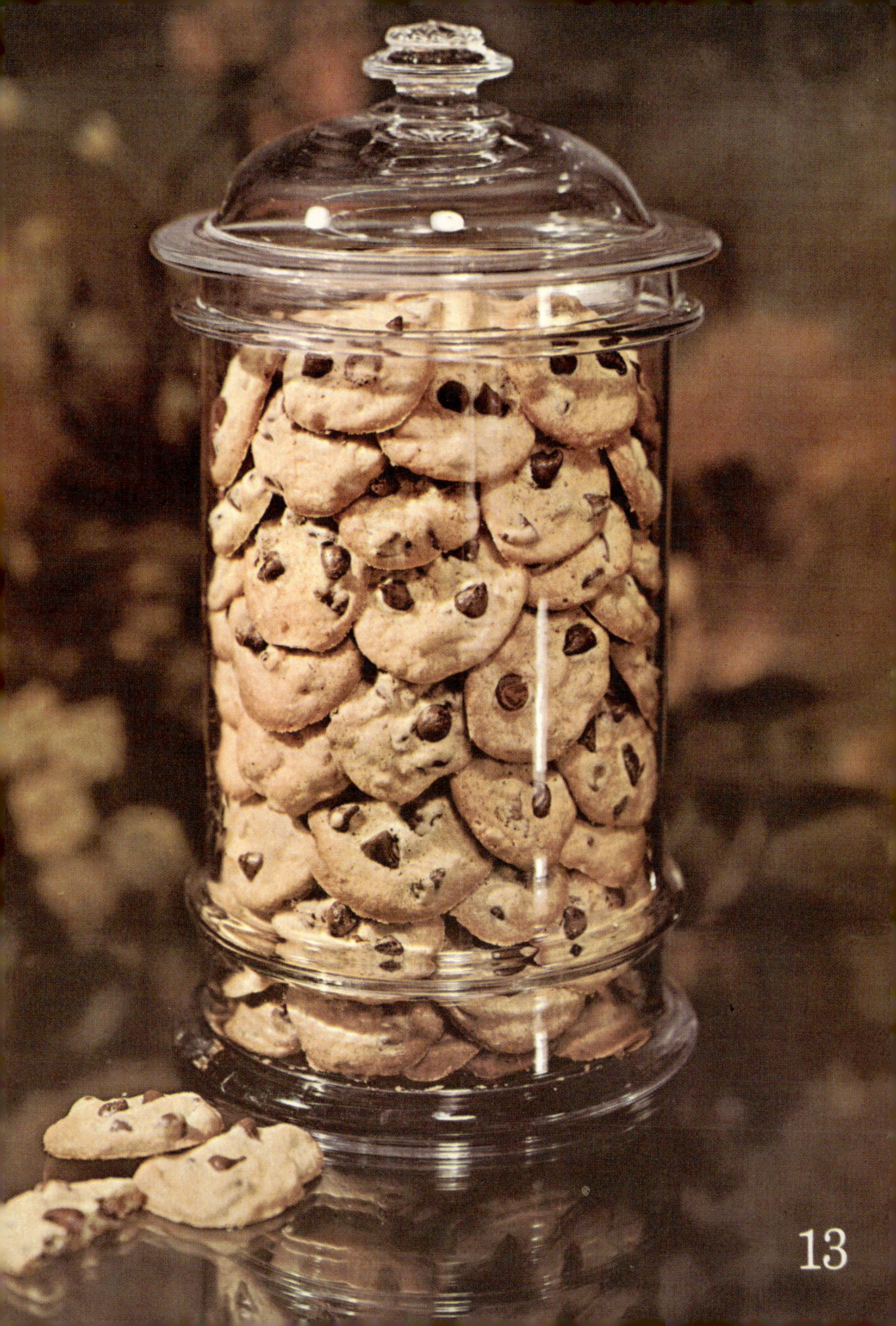

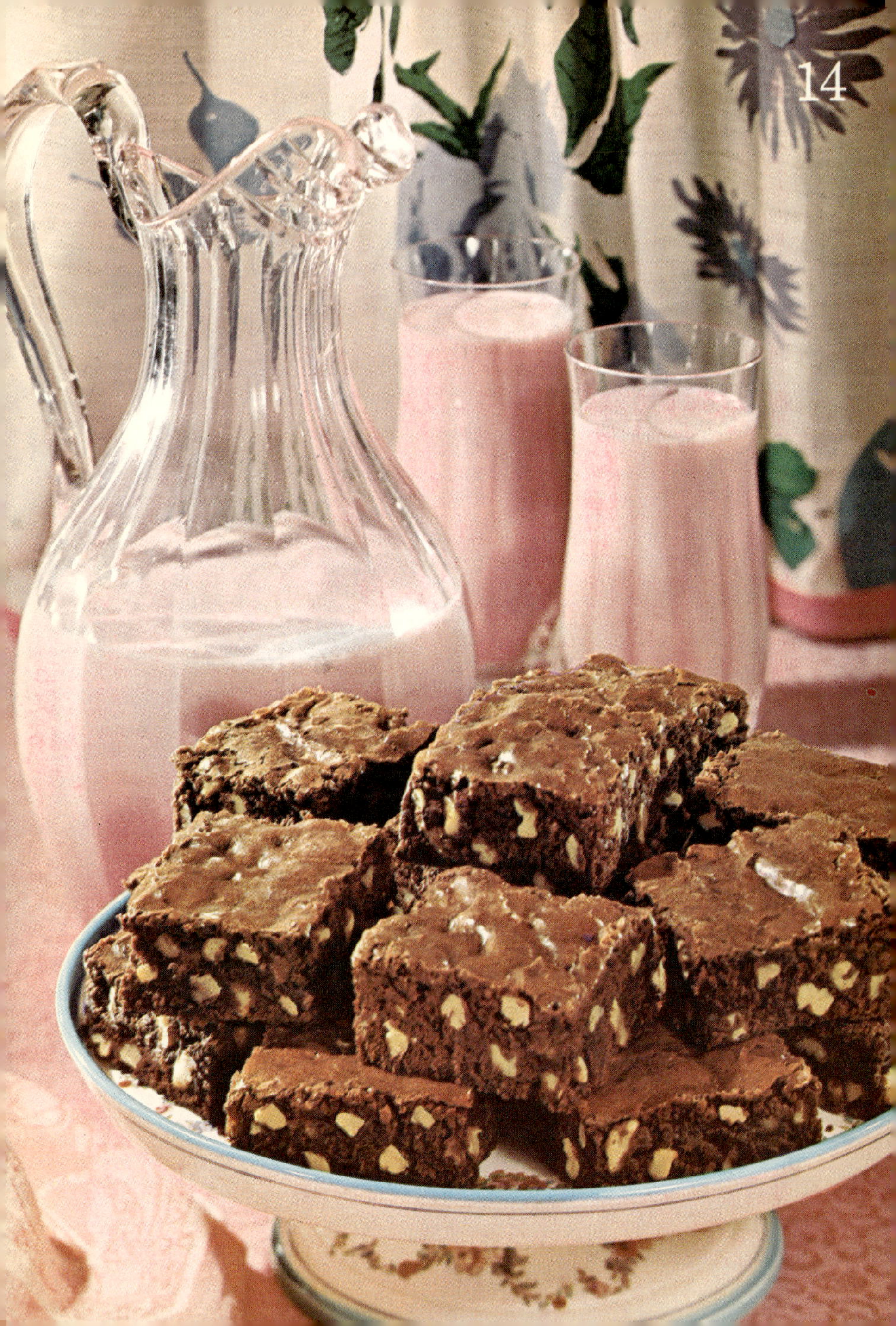

BUTTERSCOTCH SNAPS

Preheat oven to 350°F.

SIFT together and set aside
  2 c. sifted flour
  2 tsp. baking soda
  ¼ tsp. salt

MELT over hot (not boiling) water
  1 6-oz. pkg. (1 c.)
    Butterscotch Morsels

Remove from water

COMBINE and beat till creamy
  ½ c. sugar
  ⅓ c. butter or shortening
  3 tbs. light corn syrup

BEAT in
  1 egg

STIR in
  Melted butterscotch

ADD
  Flour mixture

Form in 1″ balls

ROLL in
  Granulated sugar

Place on greased cookie sheet

BAKE at: 350°F.

TIME: 10 min.

YIELD: approx. 5 dozen

Note: To keep crisp, store in tightly covered container

BUTTERSCOTCH COCONUT DROPS

Preheat oven to 375°F.

SIFT together and set aside
  2 c. sifted flour
  ½ tsp. baking soda
  ½ tsp. salt

COMBINE and beat till creamy
  ½ c. butter
  ½ c. firmly packed brown sugar
  ½ c. granulated sugar

ADD and beat till light
  2 eggs
  1 tsp. vanilla

STIR in gradually
  Flour mixture

ADD and mix well
  1 6-oz. pkg. (1 c.)
    Butterscotch Morsels
  ½ c. chopped pecans

Chill

DROP by rounded teaspoonfuls into
  1½ c. flaked coconut

Roll to coat

Form into balls

Place on greased cookie sheet

Top each with pecan half

BAKE at: 375°F.

TIME: 10 to 12 min.

YIELD: approx. 4½ dozen

SCOTCH-OAT PRIZES

Preheat oven to 350°F.

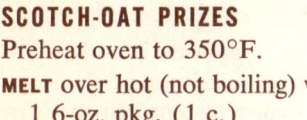

MELT over hot (not boiling) water
1 6-oz. pkg. (1 c.)
    Butterscotch Morsels
Remove from water. Let cool
approx. 10 min.

SIFT together and set aside
1 c. sifted flour
½ tsp. baking soda
½ tsp. salt

COMBINE and beat till creamy
¾ c. sugar
½ c. shortening
1 egg
1 tsp. grated orange rind

ADD and stir till blended
1 c. quick-cooking rolled oats
1 c. flaked coconut
Flour mixture
Melted butterscotch

Shape in 1″ balls. Place on greased
cookie sheet. Flatten with tines of
fork

BAKE at: 350°F.

TIME: approx. 15 min.

YIELD: approx. 5 dozen

BUTTERSCOTCH OATMEAL CRISPS

Preheat oven to 300°F.

SIFT together and set aside
½ c. sifted flour
1 tsp. baking powder
¼ tsp. salt

MELT over hot (not boiling) water
1 6-oz. pkg. (1 c.)
    Butterscotch Morsels
Remove from water

STIR in till smooth
⅓ c. vegetable shortening

BEAT in
1 egg

STIR in
Flour mixture
1 c. rolled oats

Drop by half teaspoonfuls on ungreased cookie sheet, 3″ apart, to
allow for spreading

BAKE at: 300°F.

TIME: 18 to 20 min.

Remove *immediately* from cookie
sheet. If cookies should stick, return
to oven for a few minutes

YIELD: approx. 5 dozen

STRAWBERRY KISSES
Preheat oven to 350°F.
BEAT till soft peaks form
   3 egg whites
BEAT in gradually
   ¾ c. sugar
   ¼ c. Nestlé's Strawberry Quik
Continue to beat till stiff, glossy peaks form
FOLD in
   ⅓ c. crushed salted crackers
   1 tsp. grated lemon rind
Drop by rounded teaspoonfuls on greased and floured cookie sheet
BAKE at: 350°F.
TIME: approx. 15 min.*
Cool thoroughly, before removing from cookie sheets
        YIELD: approx. 5½ dozen
*Bake till they will lift easily from sheet

CHOCO-NUT WHIZZERS
Preheat oven to 375°F.
MELT over hot (not boiling) water
   2 6-oz. pkgs. or 1 12-oz. pkg.
      (2 c.) Semi-Sweet Chocolate Morsels
Remove from water
STIR in—*do not beat*
   ⅔ c. sweetened condensed milk
   1 tbs. water
   1 tsp. vanilla
ADD
   1 c. finely chopped nuts
Drop by rounded tablespoonfuls, 2" apart, on foil-lined cookie sheet
PLACE on each cookie
   Walnut or pecan half
BAKE at: 375°F.
TIME: 10 min.
Cool thoroughly before removing from foil
        YIELD: 2 dozen

MOLASSES DANDIES
Preheat oven to 350°F.
SIFT together and set aside
   2½ c. sifted flour
   1 tsp. baking soda
   ½ tsp. cinnamon
   ¼ tsp. salt
   ⅛ tsp. ginger
COMBINE and beat till light
   ½ c. shortening
   ½ c. sugar
BEAT in
   1 egg
ADD and mix well
   Flour mixture
      alternately with
   ½ c. light molasses
   ½ c. sour milk
STIR in
   1 6-oz. pkg. (1 c.) Semi-Sweet Chocolate Morsels
Drop by tablespoonfuls on greased cookie sheet
BAKE at: 350°F.
TIME: 15 min.
Remove from cookie sheet immediately
        YIELD: approx. 3½ dozen
        2½" cookies

page 84 / cookies

CHOCOLATE PEANUT BUTTER OAT COOKIES

Preheat oven to 375°F.

SIFT together and set aside
1½ c. sifted flour
1 tsp. salt
½ tsp. baking soda

BLEND
½ c. shortening
½ c. chunk-style peanut butter
½ tsp. cinnamon
¼ tsp. nutmeg

BEAT in gradually
1 c. sugar

BEAT in, one at a time
2 eggs

ADD
Flour mixture
alternately with
½ c. water

STIR in
1 6-oz. pkg. (1 c.) Semi-Sweet
Chocolate Morsels
1 c. rolled oats

Drop by heaping teaspoonfuls on ungreased cookie sheet

BAKE at: 375°F.

TIME: 12 min.

Remove from cookie sheet at once

YIELD: approx. 5 dozen
(See illustration 8)

CRINKLY PUFFS

Preheat oven to 375°F.

MELT over hot (not boiling) water
1 12-oz. pkg. (2 c.) Semi-Sweet
Chocolate Morsels
Remove from water

STIR in
½ c. shortening
½ tsp. salt

BEAT till thick
3 eggs

BEAT in gradually till *very* thick
¾ c. sugar

ADD
1 c. quick-cooking rolled oats
Semi-sweet mixture
1 tsp. vanilla

Drop by rounded teaspoonfuls on greased cookie sheet

BAKE at: 375°F.

TIME: 6 to 8 min.

YIELD: approx. 6 dozen

Note: This recipe does not require leavening
(See illustration 8)

MERINGUE SURPRISES

Preheat oven to 300°F.

COMBINE and beat till stiff but not dry
2 egg whites
1 tsp. vanilla
⅛ tsp. salt

BEAT in gradually till stiff and satiny
½ c. sugar

FOLD in
1 6-oz. pkg. (1 c.) Semi-Sweet
Chocolate Morsels

Drop by teaspoonfuls on greased cookie sheet

BAKE at: 300°F.

TIME: 30 min.

YIELD: approx. 3½ dozen

CORN FLAKE MERINGOONS

Preheat oven to 350°F.

BEAT till stiff but not dry
- 2 egg whites
- ¼ tsp. salt
- ½ tsp. vanilla

BEAT in gradually
- 1 c. sifted confectioners' sugar

FOLD in
- 1 6-oz. pkg. (1 c.) Semi-Sweet Chocolate Morsels
- 1 c. shredded coconut
- 2 c. corn flakes

Drop by teaspoonfuls on well greased cookie sheet

BAKE at: 350°F.

TIME: 18 to 20 min.

YIELD: 3 dozen

(See illustration 9)

CRUNCHY SANDWICH COOKIES

Preheat oven to 350°F.

SIFT together and set aside
- 1 c. sifted flour
- ½ tsp. baking soda
- ¼ tsp. salt

COMBINE and beat till light and creamy
- ½ c. granulated sugar
- ½ c. firmly packed brown sugar
- ½ c. shortening

BLEND in
- 1 egg
- ½ tsp. vanilla

STIR in
- Flour mixture

ADD and stir till blended
- 1 c. cornflakes, crushed
- 1 c. quick-cooking rolled oats
- ½ c. coconut

REMOVE and reserve
- ⅓ of dough

Shape remaining ⅔ of dough into balls using level teaspoonfuls for each. Place on greased cookie sheets. Flatten with bottom of glass dipped in flour

BAKE at: 350°F.

TIME: 8 to 10 min.

Shape reserved ⅓ of dough into balls, using half teaspoonfuls for each

Place on greased cookie sheets

BAKE at: 350°F.

TIME: 8 min.

Cool

Prepare

CHOCOLATE FILLING

MELT over hot (not boiling) water
- 1 6-oz. pkg. (1 c.) Semi-Sweet Chocolate Morsels
- ½ c. sifted confectioners' sugar
- 1 tbs. water

BLEND in and beat till smooth
- 1 3-oz. pkg. soft cream cheese

Cool

Spread Chocolate Filling on larger cookies and top with small ones

YIELD: 3½ dozen

(See illustration 9)

page 86 / cookies

CHOCOLATE CRISPS

Preheat oven to 375°F.

SIFT together and set aside
2 c. sifted flour
½ tsp. baking soda
½ tsp. salt

COMBINE and beat till creamy
1½ c. sugar
1 c. soft butter or margarine

ADD and beat well
2 eggs
1 tsp. vanilla

STIR in
1 c. ready-to-eat shredded
bran cereal
1 6-oz. pkg. (1 c.) Semi-Sweet
Chocolate Morsels

ADD and mix well
Flour mixture

Drop by teaspoonfuls onto
ungreased cookie sheet

BAKE at: 375°F.
TIME: 12 min.

YIELD: 6½ dozen

CHOCOLATE BANANA COOKIES

Preheat oven to 400°F.

MELT over hot (not boiling) water
1 6-oz. pkg. (1 c.) Semi-Sweet
Chocolate Morsels

SIFT together and set aside
2¼ c. sifted flour
2 tsp. baking powder
½ tsp. salt
¼ tsp. baking soda

COMBINE and beat till creamy
1 c. firmly packed brown sugar
⅔ c. shortening

BEAT in, one at a time
2 eggs

ADD and mix well
Flour mixture
2 fully-ripe bananas,
mashed (1 c.)
Melted semi-sweet
1 tsp. grated lemon rind

Drop by teaspoonfuls on greased
cookie sheet

BAKE at: 400°F.
TIME: 10 min.

YIELD: approx. 7 dozen

MOCHA PECAN BUTTONS

Preheat oven to 375°F.

MELT over hot (not boiling) water
1 6-oz. pkg. (1 c.) Semi-Sweet
Chocolate Morsels
Remove from water

Cool approx. 5 min.

BEAT till thick
2 eggs

BEAT in gradually till *very* thick
½ c. sugar

COMBINE and stir in
2 tbs. flour
1 tsp. baking powder
1 tsp. Nescafé
⅛ tsp. salt

ADD and mix well
Cooled semi-sweet

Drop by half teaspoonfuls on
greased cookie sheet

Place 1 pecan half in center of
each cookie

BAKE at: 375°F.
TIME: 6 to 8 min.

YIELD: approx. 6 dozen

CHOCO-ORANGE OATIES

Preheat oven to 375°F.

SIFT together and set aside
- 1 c. sifted flour
- 1 tsp. salt

COMBINE and beat till creamy
- 1 c. firmly packed brown sugar
- ½ c. soft butter

ADD and beat till light
- 1 egg
- 1 tsp. grated orange rind
- 1 tsp. vanilla

STIR in gradually
- Flour mixture

ADD and mix well
- 1 6-oz. pkg. (1 c.) Semi-Sweet Chocolate Morsels
- 1 c. rolled oats
- 1 c. coarsely chopped nuts

Drop by heaping teaspoonfuls on ungreased cookie sheet

BAKE at: 375°F.

TIME: approx. 12 min.

Remove from cookie sheet immediately

YIELD: approx. 4 dozen

STRAWBERRY COOKIES

Preheat oven to 350°F.

SIFT together and set aside
- 2 c. sifted flour
- 2 tsp. baking powder
- ½ tsp. salt

COMBINE and beat till creamy
- ⅔ c. shortening
- ⅔ c. sugar
- ⅓ c. Nestlé's Strawberry Quik

ADD and beat till well blended
- 1 egg
- 1 tbs. lemon juice

ADD and mix well
- Flour mixture

Roll dough to ⅛" thickness on floured board. Cut in desired shapes with cookie cutters

Place on ungreased cookie sheet

BAKE at: 350°F.

TIME: 8 to 10 min.

YIELD: approx. 3 dozen*

Cover with Chocolate Glaze *(see page 21)* and decorate with Strawberry Butter Frosting *(see page 26)*, if desired

*To store in freezer: Wrap in foil and freeze, before frosting.

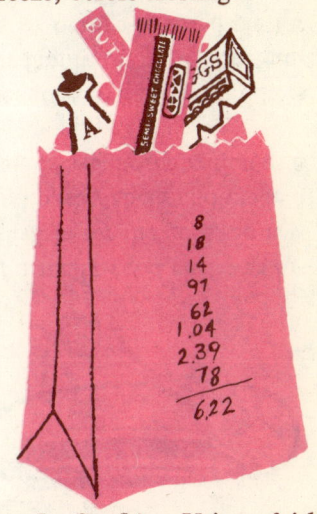

Namesake Cookies: Using a fairly thin decorating tube, spell out names on large cookies for a birthday party special. Faces are fun, too, children love to take them home as souvenirs. Add a stick while the cookie is still warm, if you like, for unusual pops.

(See illustration 26)

Pie Making Is an Art

The great Escoffier once said that the test of a really good chef was his ability to transform an ordinary stew into a dish fit for the gods. So it is with pies. Once a woman has mastered a good pastry shell, and made a few wonderful pies of her own, she can gain an overnight reputation as a gourmet's cook.

Our first pies are luxurious chocolate beauties. We go on to others sure to become clamored-for favorites of your family. At your next Sunday dinner, for a change of pace, try a mint- or orange-flavored pie for delighted "bravos" from family and guests alike. On that particular occasion when nothing but the most spectacular will do, Heavenly Cheese Pie makes a most impressive showing.

You'll be thrilled with the very special pie-crusts in this chapter, too. There are a chocolate nut, rich and crunchy; a meringue which melts on your tongue; some that require no baking at all. Each is fool-proof and an easy-to-follow recipe. Tender loving care, perfect ingredients, and the willingness to invest extra time to learn the simple steps, are all it takes to turn out pies you'll be proud to serve anyone, anytime.

Whether you are entertaining at an elegant party, or simply cooking for a family-at-home dinner, treat the pies you have so lovingly made as something truly special. They will make any meal an occasion.

We know these pie recipes will light a spark, start your imagination working, and help you to turn out masterpieces.

Prize Chocolate Pies

DELICIOUS CHOCOLATE PIE
SHELL
Have ready 1 baked and cooled 8" pie shell

FILLING
COMBINE in a saucepan
- 1 c. Nestlé's EverReady Cocoa
- ¼ c. sugar
- 4 tbs. cornstarch
- ⅛ tsp. salt

ADD gradually, stirring till smooth
- 1½ c. milk

Bring to a boil over low heat, stirring constantly. Continue cooking till thick, stirring constantly

Remove from heat

Cover tightly. Cool to room temperature. Stir till smooth

FOLD in
- ½ c. heavy cream, whipped

Pour into prepared pie shell

Chill till set

BLACK BOTTOM PIE
Have ready 1 baked 9" pie shell

COMBINE in heavy saucepan
- 1¼ tbs. cornstarch
- ½ c. sugar
- 4 egg yolks, beaten

ADD gradually
- 2 c. scalded milk

Cook, stirring until mixture coats spoon

ADD and beat till well blended
- 1 c. cooked mixture
- 1 6-oz. pkg. (1 c.) Nestlé's Semi-Sweet Chocolate Morsels
- ½ tsp. vanilla

Pour into baked pie shell

COMBINE and let stand 5 min.
- 1 envelope unflavored gelatin
- ¼ c. cold water
- ½ tsp. vanilla

ADD to remaining hot, cooked mixture
- Gelatin mixture

Stir till gelatin dissolves

Cool

COMBINE and beat till foamy
- 4 egg whites
- ¼ tsp. cream of tartar

ADD gradually and continue beating till stiff and glossy
- ½ c. sugar

Fold into gelatin mixture

Pour over semi-sweet mixture in pie shell

Chill till set

Garnish with whipped cream, if desired

MOCHA ANGEL PIE

Preheat oven to 275°F.

MERINGUE PIE SHELL

BEAT till stiff but not dry
3 egg whites

BEAT in gradually till stiff and satiny
¾ c. sugar
Dash salt

Spread approx. ⅔ of meringue on bottom and sides (not rim) of well-greased 8″ pie pan. Drop remaining meringue in mounds around rim of pan

BAKE at: 275°F.
TIME: 1 hr.
Cool
Prepare

FILLING

COMBINE and bring just to boil, stirring constantly
⅓ c. light corn syrup
⅓ c. water
1 tbs. Nescafé

Remove from heat

STIR in till smooth
1 12-oz. pkg. (2 c.) Semi-Sweet Chocolate Morsels

BEAT in, one at a time
3 egg yolks

Cool approx. 10 min.

FOLD in
1 c. heavy cream, whipped
1 tsp. vanilla

Pour in cooled Meringue Shell. Chill several hours or overnight
(See illustration 18)

FLUFFY CHOCOLATE-RICE PIE

Have ready 1 baked and cooled 9″ pie shell

COMBINE in saucepan and mix well
¼ c. sugar
1 envelope unflavored gelatin
¼ tsp. salt

ADD and bring *just* to boil over moderate heat, stirring constantly
2 c. cooked, regular rice
½ c. cold water
1 egg, slightly beaten

Remove from heat

ADD and stir till melted
1 6-oz. pkg. (1 c.) Semi-Sweet Chocolate Morsels

STIR in gradually
½ c. water

ADD
¼ c. mixed candied fruit, finely chopped

FOLD in
1 c. heavy cream, whipped

Chill, stirring occasionally, till mixture begins to hold its shape

Spoon into prepared shell

Chill several hours or overnight

MOCHA BISQUE PIE

Have ready 1 baked 9" pie shell

COMBINE and melt over moderate heat, stirring constantly
- ¼ lb. (16) marshmallows
- ½ c. water
- 1 tbs. Nescafé
- ½ tsp. salt

BEAT slightly
- 2 egg yolks

ADD gradually, stirring rapidly
- Nescafé mixture

Cook over moderate heat 1 min., stirring constantly

Cool approx. 10 min.

FOLD in
- ¾ c. heavy cream, whipped

Freeze till firm

COMBINE and melt over hot (not boiling) water
- 1 6-oz. pkg. (1 c.) Semi-Sweet Chocolate Morsels
- 1 tbs. shortening

COMBINE and beat till stiff but not dry
- 2 egg whites
- 1 tsp. vanilla
- ¼ tsp. almond extract

BEAT in gradually till stiff and glossy
- 1 c. firmly packed brown sugar

PLACE in chilled bowl and stir till smooth, but not melted
- Frozen mixture

Pour over, in thin stream, stirring constantly, to form "flecks"
- Melted chocolate

FOLD in
- Egg-white mixture

Pour in pie shell

Freeze till firm

CHOCOLATE PECAN PIE

Preheat oven to 350°F.

SHELL

GREASE bottom and sides (not rim) of 8" pie pan with
- 1 tbs. soft butter

PRESS gently in butter
- ¾ c. pecans, finely chopped

FILLING

MELT over hot (not boiling) water
- 1 6-oz. pkg. (1 c.) Semi-Sweet Chocolate Morsels

Remove from water

COMBINE and beat well
- ½ c. dark corn syrup
- 2 eggs
- 1 tsp. vanilla
- ¼ tsp. salt

ADD slowly, stirring rapidly
- Melted semi-sweet

Pour in prepared Shell

SPRINKLE over Filling
- ¼ c. pecans, coarsely chopped

BAKE at: 350°F.

TIME: 25 to 30 min.

Serve warm or cold

page 92 / pies

CHOCOLATE ALMOND PIE

SHELL

Line a 9″ pie pan with aluminum foil

MELT over hot (not boiling) water
   ½ 9¾-oz. Nestlé's Milk
      Chocolate Bar
   1 tsp. cooking or salad oil
Stir till smooth

ADD and stir till well blended
   1 c. finely chopped nuts
Spread evenly on bottom and sides (not over rim) of prepared pie pan

Chill till firm. Lift out of pan. Peel off foil. Replace chocolate shell in pie pan

FILLING

COMBINE over hot (not boiling) water and stir to blend
   ¼ lb. (16) marshmallows
   ½ 9¾-oz. Nestlé's Milk
      Chocolate Bar
   ¼ c. milk
   1 tsp. vanilla
   ¼ tsp. almond extract

Remove from water

Cool

FOLD in
   1 c. heavy cream, whipped
Pour into prepared Shell

Chill at least 2 hours

BROWNIE PIE

SHELL

Have ready 1 unbaked 9″ pie shell
Preheat oven to 350°F.

FILLING

COMBINE and bring *just* to boil over moderate heat, stirring constantly
   1 14-oz. can (1¼ c.)
      sweetened condensed milk
   ¼ tsp. salt

STIR in till smooth
   1 6-oz. pkg. (1 c.) Semi-Sweet
      Chocolate Morsels
   2 tbs. flour
   1 tsp. vanilla

BEAT in, one at a time
   2 egg yolks

STIR in
   ½ c. chopped nuts, if desired

BEAT till stiff, but not dry
   2 egg whites

BEAT in till stiff, glossy peaks form
   2 tbs. sugar

FOLD into semi-sweet mixture
   Egg white mixture
Pour in prepared Shell

BAKE at: 350°F.

TIME: 40 to 45 min.

Serve warm, or cool—with whipped cream, if desired

EASY-DO PIE
SHELL
Have ready 1 unbaked 9″ pie shell
Preheat oven to 350°F.

FILLING
MELT over hot (not boiling) water
    1 6-oz. pkg. (1 c.) Semi-Sweet Chocolate Morsels

COMBINE
    1 14-oz. can (1¼ c.) sweetened condensed milk
    2 egg yolks, slightly beaten
    ¼ tsp. salt

ADD slowly, stirring rapidly
    Melted semi-sweet

BEAT till stiff but not dry
    2 egg whites

BEAT in till stiff, glossy peaks form
    2 tbs. sugar

FOLD into semi-sweet mixture
    Egg white mixture
Pour in prepared Shell

BAKE at: 350°F.

TIME: 35 min.

Serve warm or cold

Note: Upon cooling, Filling has slight tendency to crack

Dreamy Creams and Heavenly Chiffons

MOCHA CREAM PIE
SHELL
Have ready one 9″ Choco-Nut Shell *(see page 97)*

FILLING
COMBINE and place over hot (not boiling) water till semi-sweet melts
    1 6-oz. pkg. (1 c.) Semi-Sweet Chocolate Morsels
    ¼ c. water
    4 tsp. Nescafé
    ⅛ tsp. salt

Stir till blended and smooth

Remove from hot water. Turn into mixing bowl

STIR in
    1 7½-oz. jar marshmallow cream

BEAT till stiff but not dry
    2 egg whites

FOLD in
    1 c. heavy cream, whipped
    1 tsp. vanilla
    ¼ tsp. almond extract

ADD and fold in gently, till well blended
    Semi-sweet mixture
Pile into Choco-Nut Shell

Chill till firm

Garnish with whipped cream, if desired

CAFÉ BUTTERSCOTCH CHIFFON PIE

SHELL

Have ready 1 baked and cooled 9″ pie shell

FILLING

COMBINE and cook over moderate heat till gelatin dissolves and mixture comes to boil, stirring constantly
- ½ c. cold water
- 1 envelope unflavored gelatin
- 4 tsp. Nescafé
- ¼ tsp. salt

Remove from heat

BEAT slightly
- 2 egg yolks

ADD gradually, stirring rapidly
- Nescafé mixture

Cook over low heat 1 min., stirring constantly

Remove from heat

STIR in
- 1 6-oz. pkg. (1 c.) Nestlé's Butterscotch Morsels

BEAT till stiff but not dry
- 2 egg whites

BEAT in till stiff, glossy peaks form
- ½ c. firmly packed brown sugar

FOLD in
- Butterscotch mixture
- 1 c. heavy cream, whipped
- 1 tsp. grated orange rind

Pour in prepared Shell

Chill

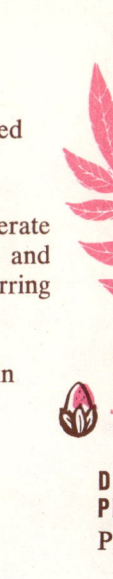

DEEP SOUTH BUTTERSCOTCH PECAN PIE

Preheat oven to 350°F.

SHELL

PREPARE and place in pan
- Pastry for one 8″ pie shell

FILLING

MELT over hot (not boiling) water
- 1 6-oz. pkg. (1 c.) Butterscotch Morsels

Remove from water

COMBINE and beat well
- ½ c. corn syrup
- 2 eggs
- ¼ tsp. salt

ADD slowly, stirring rapidly
- Melted butterscotch

ADD
- ½ c. pecan halves

Pour into prepared Shell

BAKE at: 350°F.

TIME: 45 min.

Serve warm or cool with whipped cream, if desired

(See illustration 16)

BUTTERSCOTCH CHIFFON PIE
SHELL
Have ready 1 baked and cooled 9" pie shell

FILLING
COMBINE and let stand 5 min.
 ½ c. cold water
 1 envelope unflavored gelatin
 ¼ tsp. salt

Stir over moderate heat till gelatin dissolves and mixture comes to boil

Remove from heat

BEAT slightly
 4 egg yolks

ADD gradually, stirring rapidly
 Gelatin mixture

Cook over low heat 1 min., stirring constantly

Remove from heat

ADD and stir till smooth
 1 6-oz. pkg. (1 c.)
  Butterscotch Morsels

BEAT till stiff but not dry
 4 egg whites

ADD gradually, beating till stiff and glossy
 ½ c. sugar

FOLD in
 Butterscotch mixture

Pour into prepared Shell. Chill several hours or overnight

ORANGE CREAM PIE
Preheat oven to 275°F.

MERINGUE PIE SHELL
BEAT till stiff but not dry
 3 egg whites

BEAT in gradually till stiff and satiny
 ¾ c. sugar
 Dash salt

FOLD in
 Grated rind of 1 orange

Spread approx. ⅔ of meringue on bottom and sides (not rim) of well-greased 8" pie pan. Drop remaining meringue in mounds around rim of pan

BAKE at: 275°F.

TIME: 1 hr.

Cool. Fill with

FILLING
COMBINE and melt over moderate heat, stirring constantly
 ¼ lb. (16) marshmallows
 ⅓ c. orange juice

Remove from heat

STIR in till melted
 1 6-oz. pkg. (1 c.) Semi-Sweet Chocolate Morsels

BEAT in, one at a time
 3 egg yolks

FOLD in
 1 c. heavy cream, whipped
 1 tsp. vanilla

Pour in cooled Meringue Shell

Chill several hours or overnight

page 95 / pies

GOLD COAST CHIFFON PIE
SHELL
Have ready 1 baked and cooled 9″ pie shell

FILLING
COMBINE in saucepan
  ⅔ c. sugar
  1 envelope unflavored gelatin
  ¼ tsp. salt

COMBINE and mix well
  1½ c. milk
  1 c. Nestlé's EverReady Cocoa

STIR into gelatin mixture
  EverReady mixture

Cook over moderate heat, stirring constantly, till gelatin dissolves and mixture just comes to a boil

Remove from heat

Chill, stirring occasionally till thickened but not set

FOLD in
  ½ c. heavy cream, whipped
  1 tsp. vanilla

Pour into prepared shell

Chill

NESCAFÉ CREAM PIE
NUT SHELL
Preheat oven to 400°F.

COMBINE and beat till stiff but not dry
  1 egg white
  ⅛ tsp. salt

BEAT in gradually till stiff, glossy peaks form
  ¼ c. sugar

ADD and blend well
  1½ c. finely chopped nuts

Press on bottom and sides (not rim) of a well greased 8″ pie pan

Prick well with fork

BAKE at: 400°F.

TIME: 12 min.

Cool

FILLING
COMBINE and melt over medium heat, stirring constantly
  ¼ lb. (16) marshmallows
  ¼ c. water
  1 tbs. Nescafé

BEAT slightly
  1 egg yolk

ADD slowly, stirring rapidly
  Nescafé mixture

Cook over medium heat for 1 min., stirring constantly

Chill till thickened but not set

Beat slightly

FOLD into Nescafé mixture
  1 c. heavy cream, whipped
  ¼ tsp. almond extract

Pour into cooled shell. Chill several hours

Decorate with chopped nuts or drop small mounds of whipped cream, flavored with crème de cacao, around edge (optional)

Gala Party Pies

BAVARIAN MINT PIE
CHOCO-NUT SHELL

Line a 9" pie pan with aluminum foil

MELT over hot (not boiling) water
 1 6-oz. pkg. (1 c.) Semi-Sweet Chocolate Morsels
 1 tbs. shortening
Stir till smooth

RESERVE for Chocolate Triangles
 2 tbs. semi-sweet mixture

ADD to remaining semi-sweet mixture and stir till well blended
 1½ c. finely chopped nuts
Spread evenly on bottom and sides (not over rim) of prepared pie pan
Chill till firm. Lift out of pan. Peel off foil. Replace semi-sweet shell in pie pan

CHOCOLATE TRIANGLES

SPREAD evenly on waxed paper-lined cookie sheet to form a 6" x 4" rectangle
 Reserved 2 tbs. melted semi-sweet mixture
Chill till firm
Invert carefully on waxed paper-lined cookie sheet. Gently peel off waxed paper. Cut in 2" squares and cut each square diagonally to make triangles. Chill till ready to use

FILLING

COMBINE and melt over hot water
 ½ lb. (32) marshmallows
 ¾ c. milk
 ¼ tsp. salt
Remove from water. Cool

ADD and stir till blended
 ¼ tsp. peppermint extract

FOLD in
 1¼ c. heavy cream, whipped
 Few drops green food coloring

POUR into
 Chilled Choco-Nut Shell
Chill several hours or overnight
Garnish by pressing the long side of the Chocolate Triangles into the top (so that they stand up)
 (See illustration 16)

APPLESAUCE PIE
SHELL
Have ready 1 baked and cooled 9″ pie shell
FILLING
COMBINE in saucepan
  1 envelope unflavored gelatin
  ¼ c. sugar or firmly packed brown sugar
  ⅛ tsp. salt
ADD and mix well
  1½ c. canned applesauce (approx. 1-lb. can)
  2 egg yolks
  ⅛ tsp. cinnamon
Bring *just* to boil, over moderate heat, stirring constantly
Remove from heat
STIR in till melted
  1 6-oz. pkg. (1 c.) Semi-Sweet Chocolate Morsels
BLEND in
  1 14½-oz. can (1⅔ c.) evaporated milk, undiluted
  1 tsp. vanilla
Chill till slightly thickened
BEAT till stiff but not dry
  2 egg whites
BEAT in gradually till stiff, glossy peaks form
  ¼ c. sugar or firmly packed brown sugar
FOLD in
  Chilled semi-sweet mixture
Pour in prepared Shell. Chill several hours or overnight

MARBLE DELIGHT PIE
SHELL
Have ready 1 baked and cooled 9″ pie shell
FILLING
Part 1
COMBINE in saucepan
  ½ lb. (32) marshmallows
  ⅓ c. water
  ¼ tsp. salt
Place over moderate heat, and stir constantly till marshmallows melt
Remove from heat
RESERVE
  ¾ c. marshmallow mixture
ADD to remaining marshmallow mixture, and stir till melted
  1 6-oz. pkg. (1 c.) Semi-Sweet Chocolate Morsels
BEAT in
  2 egg yolks
FOLD in
  1 c. heavy cream, whipped
  Few drops almond extract
Pour into cooled Shell
Part 2
BEAT till stiff but not dry
  2 egg whites
BEAT in gradually till stiff and glossy
  Reserved ¾ c. marshmallow mixture
SPREAD over
  Semi-sweet mixture
Fold egg-white mixture gently into semi-sweet mixture to marbleize
Chill several hours

MEDITERRANEAN PIE
SHELL

Add 2 tbs. sesame seeds with the water when preparing dough for one 8" pie shell. Bake according to recipe directions. Let cool

FILLING

MELT over hot (not boiling) water
    1 6-oz. pkg. (1 c.) Semi-Sweet Chocolate Morsels

Remove from water

BEAT in
    2 egg yolks

STIR in gradually till smooth
    2 tbs. water

ADD and mix well
    1 c. commercial sour cream
    ¼ tsp. salt

BEAT till stiff but not dry
    2 egg whites

BEAT in gradually till stiff, glossy peaks form
    ⅓ c. honey

FOLD in
    Semi-sweet mixture

Pour into cooled Shell

SPRINKLE over top
    2 tbs. toasted sesame seeds

Chill several hours or overnight

HEAVENLY CHEESE PIE
SHELL

COMBINE
    1½ c. graham cracker crumbs
    ⅓ c. butter, melted
    ¼ c. firmly packed brown sugar
    ⅛ tsp. nutmeg

Reserve 2 tbs. for topping

Press remaining crumb mixture on bottom and sides (not rim) of 9" pie pan

Chill while preparing filling

FILLING

MELT over hot (not boiling) water
    1 6-oz. pkg. (1 c.) Semi-Sweet Chocolate Morsels

Cool approx. 10 min.

BLEND
    1 8-oz. pkg. soft cream cheese
    ½ c. firmly packed brown sugar
    ⅛ tsp. salt

BEAT in, one at a time
    2 egg yolks

STIR in
    Cooled semi-sweet

BEAT till stiff but not dry
    2 egg whites

BEAT in gradually till stiff, glossy peaks form
    ¼ c. firmly packed brown sugar

FOLD into semi-sweet mixture
    Egg white mixture
    1 c. heavy cream, whipped
    1 tsp. vanilla

Pour into chilled Shell

SPRINKLE over top
    Reserved crumb mixture

Chill several hours or overnight

page 100 | pies

LAYERED ALASKAN PIE
SHELL

Have ready 1 baked and cooled
9″ pie shell

Prepare
FUDGE SAUCE

COMBINE in a saucepan and simmer
till sugar is dissolved
- ¾ c. sugar
- ½ c. evaporated milk

Bring to a *full* boil and remove
from heat

ADD and stir till blended and smooth
- 1 6-oz. pkg. (1 c.) Semi-Sweet
  Chocolate Morsels
- 1 tsp. vanilla

Cool to room temperature

RESERVE for glaze
- 2 tbs. Fudge Sauce

FILLING

SPREAD in prepared Shell
- 1 pt. softened vanilla ice cream

COVER with
- ½ of Fudge Sauce

Freeze

SPREAD with second layer of
- 1 pt. softened vanilla ice cream

TOP with
- Remaining ½ of Fudge Sauce

Freeze

Prepare

MERINGUE

Preheat oven to 475°F.

COMBINE and beat till stiff, glossy
peaks form
- 3 egg whites
- ½ c. sugar
- ⅛ tsp. cream of tartar

SPREAD over pie, sealing edges well
- Meringue mixture

SPRINKLE on top
- 1 tbs. crushed peppermint
  stick candy

BAKE at: 475°F.

TIME: approx. 4 min.

Prepare

GLAZE

REHEAT over low heat
- Reserved 2 tbs. Fudge Sauce
- 1 tsp. light corn syrup
- 1 tsp. water

Drizzle over top of meringue just
before serving

EASY NESSELRODE PIE

SHELL

Preheat oven to 350°F.

PLACE in 8″ pie pan
- 1 6-oz. pkg. (1 c.) Semi-Sweet Chocolate Morsels
- 1 tbs. shortening

HEAT at: 350°F.

TIME: 2 to 3 min.

Remove from oven

STIR till blended and smooth
- Chocolate mixture

Spread over bottom of pan

Chill approx. 5 min., till chocolate mixture is slightly thickened

Spread chocolate mixture upward to edge (not top) of rim, with back of spoon, being careful to coat pan evenly

Chill

Prepare

FILLING

COOK according to package directions
- 1 pkg. vanilla pudding mix

ADD and mix well
- ½ c. finely chopped, candied fruit
- 1 tbs. light rum

Press waxed paper directly on surface of pudding

Chill till cool, approx. ½ hr.

POUR into prepared Shell
- Chilled pudding

Chill several hours

Garnish with whipped cream, if desired, at serving time

CAFÉ PUMPKIN PIE

Have ready 1 baked and cooled 9″ pie shell

COMBINE in saucepan and mix well
- 1 envelope unflavored gelatin
- ½ c. firmly packed brown sugar

ADD
- 1 No. 2 can (approx. 2 c.) pumpkin
- 1 tbs. Nescafé
- 2 egg yolks
- ⅛ tsp. salt

BLEND in till smooth
- 1 14½-oz. can (1⅔ c.) evaporated milk

Bring to boil over moderate heat, stirring constantly

Chill, stirring occasionally, till mixture is thickened but not set

BEAT till stiff but not dry
- 2 egg whites

BEAT in gradually till stiff and glossy
- ½ c. firmly packed brown sugar

FOLD in
- Pumpkin mixture
- ¼ c. crème de cacao

Pour into pie shell

Chill till set

PEACH CAROUSEL PIE

Preheat oven to 425°F.

SHELL

SIFT together into mixing bowl
  1½ c. sifted flour
  1 tsp. salt
STIR in
  ¼ c. shredded Cheddar cheese
CUT in till particles are size of
small peas
  ½ c. shortening
SPRINKLE over mixture, while toss-
ing and stirring lightly with a fork
  4 to 5 tbs. cold water

Add water to driest particles, push-
ing lumps to side, till dough is moist
enough to hold together

Form into ball. Flatten to ½″
thickness; smooth edges

Roll out on floured surface to 13″
circle. Place on foil cut to same
size. Fold up foil and dough to
make a ½″ standing rim; flute

Prepare

BUTTERSCOTCH PEACH FILLING

COMBINE and melt in saucepan,
over low heat
  ½ 6-oz. pkg. (½ c.)
    Butterscotch Morsels
  2 tbs. evaporated milk

Spread over
PLACE on pastry in petal fashion
  2 c. (1 1-lb. 13-oz. can) drained
    peach slices
SPRINKLE with
  1 tbs. lemon juice
COMBINE and sprinkle over peaches
  ½ c. chopped pecans
  ¼ c. granulated sugar
  ¼ c. firmly packed brown sugar

  1 tbs. cornstarch
  ½ tsp. cinnamon
  ½ tsp. nutmeg
GARNISH with
  ¼ c. maraschino cherry halves
BAKE at: 425°F.
TIME: 25-30 min.

Serve warm or cold with whipped
cream

TRIPLE-TREAT PIE

SHELL

Have ready 1 baked and cooled 8″
pie shell

FILLING

MELT over hot (not boiling) water
  1 6-oz. pkg. (1 c.) Semi-Sweet
    Chocolate Morsels
Remove from hot water
SPREAD on bottom of baked pie shell
  2 tbs. melted semi-sweet
BEAT into remaining semi-sweet,
one at a time
  2 egg yolks
STIR in gradually
  ¼ c. water
COMBINE and beat till stiff
  1 c. heavy cream
  ¼ c. sugar
  ¼ tsp. cinnamon
SPREAD over semi-sweet in Shell
  ½ of whipped cream mixture
SPREAD over whipped cream layer
  ½ of semi-sweet mixture
FOLD into remaining whipped
cream mixture
  Remaining semi-sweet mixture
Spread over semi-sweet layer
Chill several hours or overnight

GALA PIE

SHELL

COMBINE in saucepan and bring to boil, stirring constantly
- ¼ c. butter
- 1 tbs. water
- 4 tsp. Nescafé

Remove from heat

ADD and mix well
- 1½ c. vanilla wafer crumbs (approx. 3½ dozen wafers)

Press on bottom and sides (not rim) of greased 9" pie pan

Chill

FILLING

COMBINE
- ¼ c. sugar
- 1 envelope unflavored gelatin
- ⅛ tsp. salt

BEAT together in top of double boiler
- 1¼ c. milk
- 2 egg yolks

STIR in
- Gelatin mixture

Cook over boiling water, stirring constantly, till gelatin is dissolved —about 5 min.

Remove from water

ADD and stir till smooth
- 1 12-oz. pkg. (2 c.) Semi-Sweet Chocolate Morsels

Chill till slightly thickened

BEAT till stiff but not dry
- 2 egg whites

BEAT in gradually till stiff, glossy peaks form
- ½ c. sugar

FOLD into semi-sweet mixture
- Egg white mixture

COMBINE and beat till stiff
- 1 c. heavy cream
- ¼ c. sugar
- 1 tsp. vanilla

SPOON by tablespoonfuls in prepared Shell
- Semi-sweet mixture alternately with
- Whipped cream mixture

Chill several hours or overnight

Desserts You'll Treasure

Who can resist a cream-lavished chocolate pudding? Or a smooth vanilla dessert, with a choice of butterscotch or mocha sauce? For children, for delicate appetites, for late-at-night snacks, an on-hand bowl of flavorful dessert is the perfect answer.

Your grocer stocks many varieties of packaged puddings and mixes. *You* supply the individual touch which creates delicacies enjoyed by every member of your family. For instance, experiment for just the right flavor to spark that perennial standby, rice pudding. Try butterscotch morsels stirred in during the last fifteen minutes of baking—or chocolate morsels, spiced with a dash of cinnamon. You'll discover taste treats you never thought possible from pantry staples. And when simple vanilla pudding emerges as a chocolate-mocha-almond-flavored *parfait,* you'll have experienced the glowing satisfaction of creative cookery.

You will find an assortment of puddings and desserts in the pages that follow—including six of the most tempting guest-flattering soufflés and mousses you ever carried proudly to the table. Thanks to present-day techniques these only *look* as though they had taken hours of preparation. Our cold soufflés are foolproof, and once made, they will wait patiently in your refrigerator until served. Simple-to-follow directions should remove, once and for all, the panic that often accompanies the very thought of soufflé-preparation.

And last, there are sauces of mouth-watering richness to spoon over simple puddings, toppings to make little hands—and big ones—reach for more.

Put them all together and you have an assortment of desserts that will amply repay your happily-invested time and effort with sweet satisfaction.

Family Favorites

STRAWBERRY DESSERT ROLL

Preheat oven to 375°F.
PREPARE according to package directions
    1 pkg. angel food cake mix
Spread ½ of cake batter* in greased 15″ x 10″ x 1″ pan lined with greased waxed paper
BAKE at: 375°F.
TIME: 20 min.
Cool
Invert on towel dusted with confectioners' sugar. Remove waxed paper. Roll in towel
Prepare

FILLING

PLACE in bowl and chill
    1 c. heavy cream
    ¼ c. Nestlé's Strawberry Quik
    Dash of salt
Beat till thick
Unroll cake; spread with Filling; roll up again
Chill
Serve dusted with confectioners' sugar, if desired
                  YIELD: 12 servings
*Use remaining batter for cupcakes

3-MINUTE CHOCOLATE QUIK PUDDING

COMBINE
    ½ c. Nestlé's Chocolate Quik
    3 tbs. flour
    ¼ c. sugar
    ⅛ tsp. salt
STIR in slowly
    2 c. milk
Bring to *full* boil over moderate heat, stirring constantly
Remove from heat
BLEND in
    2 tbs. soft butter
    1 tsp. vanilla
Pour into sherbet glasses. Chill
                  YIELD: 4 servings

PETITS PUFFS CAFÉ

Have ready 16 small cream puff shells

FILLING

COMBINE and beat till stiff
    1 c. heavy cream
    ¼ c. firmly packed brown sugar
    1½ tsp. Nescafé
    ⅛ tsp. almond extract
CUT slice off tops of cream puff shells and fill with
    Filling
Chill till needed or wrap in foil and freeze
      (See illustration 19)

page 106 | desserts

COMBINE and beat till creamy
    1 3-oz. pkg. soft cream cheese
    ⅔ c. firmly packed brown sugar
    ½ tsp. vanilla
    Dash salt

BEAT in
    1 egg yolk

STIR in
    Cooled semi-sweet

FOLD in
    ¾ c. heavy cream, whipped
Spoon into custard cups
Chill

                YIELD: 6 servings
(See illustration 19)

CHOCOLATE VELVET

COMBINE and melt over hot
(not boiling water)
    2 12-oz. pkgs. (4 c.) Semi-Sweet
        Chocolate Morsels
    ½ c. water
    1 tsp. Nescafé
Stir till smooth

BLEND in
    ½ c. rum or cognac
    3 egg yolks
Remove from water
Cool

BEAT till foamy
    3 egg whites

ADD gradually and continue beating
till stiff, glossy peaks form
    2 tbs. sugar

FOLD into semi-sweet mixture
    1 c. heavy cream, whipped
    Egg white mixture
Chill at least 1 hour before serving

            YIELD: approx. 18 servings

CHOCOLATE CHARLOTTE RUSSE

SPLIT
    12 lady fingers

BRUSH cut sides with
    ½ c. orange juice

PLACE vertically around edge of
six 5-oz. custard cups
    4 prepared, split, lady fingers

FILLING

MELT over hot (not boiling) water
    1 6-oz. pkg. (1 c.) Semi-Sweet
        Chocolate Morsels
Remove from water

"LACED" CHOCOLATE BAVARIAN

COMBINE in top of double boiler and cook over hot water, stirring till gelatin is dissolved and chocolate is melted
- ½ 6-oz. pkg. (½ c.) Semi-Sweet Chocolate Morsels
- ¼ c. firmly packed brown sugar
- 2 tbs. water
- ½ envelope (1½ tsp.) unflavored gelatin

ADD and beat till blended
- 2 egg yolks
- 2 to 3 tbs. bourbon

Remove from water

BEAT till foamy
- 2 egg whites
- ⅛ tsp. salt

ADD gradually and continue beating till stiff and glossy
- ¼ c. firmly packed brown sugar

FOLD into semi-sweet mixture
- Beaten egg white mixture
- ½ c. heavy cream, whipped
- 1 c. coarsely crumbled, crisp, cinnamon-flavored wafers

Pour mixture into sherbet dishes

Chill till firm—for several hours or overnight

Serve with whipped cream, if desired

YIELD: 5 or 6 servings
(See illustration 19)

SWEET KABOB BOAT

Make boat of foil about 5″ to 6″ long

SPREAD 5 vanilla wafers with
- Jam or preserves

STAND on edge at one end of foil "boat"
- 1 prepared vanilla wafer

SPOON in on jam
- About 4 or 5 miniature marshmallows

Press in another vanilla wafer

Continue alternately with miniature marshmallows till all vanilla wafers are used

SPRINKLE over top
- Semi-Sweet Chocolate Morsels

Place foil "boat" over low fire till marshmallows and chocolate soften—approx. 10 min.

Serve warm with fork or spoon

BARBECUE SWEETWICHES

PLACE on foil 8″ x 6″
- 2 graham crackers

SPREAD one with
- Peanut butter
- then with
- Jam or jelly

TOP with
- Marshmallow cream

SPRINKLE second graham cracker with
- 1 tbs. Semi-Sweet Chocolate Morsels

Place over low fire 10 to 12 min.

Place second graham cracker, chocolate side down, on first to make sandwich

page 108 | desserts

PEACH CRISP

Preheat oven to 400°F.

DRAIN and reserve syrup
1 1-lb. 13-oz. can sliced peaches

BLEND
½ c. butter or margarine
¼ c. brown sugar
3 tsp. vanilla
⅛ tsp. salt
⅛ tsp. nutmeg

ADD and knead till coarsely crumbled
1½ c. sifted flour

PRESS on bottom of greased 9″ square pan
⅓ crumb mixture

BAKE at: 400°F.

TIME: 8 to 10 min.

SPRINKLE over
¾ 6-oz. pkg. (¾ c.) Semi-Sweet Chocolate Morsels

ARRANGE over semi-sweet
Drained peaches

SPRINKLE over peaches to cover
Remaining crumb mixture

Place about 6″ under broiler. Broil till lightly browned — about 2 to 3 min.

Cut in 3″ squares

Prepare

SAUCE

BOIL till reduced to ½ c., about 20 min.
Peach syrup
Remove from heat

ADD and stir till melted
¼ 6-oz. pkg. (¼ c.) Semi-Sweet Chocolate Morsels

Cool

FOLD in
½ c. heavy cream, whipped
Dash nutmeg

Serve warm over warm or cooled squares

YIELD: 9 servings

NAPOLEONETTES

Have ready 36 crisp, oblong, graham or sweet crackers

PREPARE
1 recipe Strawberry Butter Frosting *(see page 26)*

Spread 2 crackers with Frosting. Sandwich together and top with a third cracker

Continue like this with remaining crackers

Frost tops and sides of all cracker "Napoleonettes"

Prepare

CHOCOLATE DECORATORS' FROSTING

COMBINE and beat till well blended
2 tbs. soft butter
2 tbs. Nestlé's Chocolate Quik
¼ tsp. water

Press through small opening of pastry tube to make rippled lines on top

YIELD: 12

(See illustration 19)

PARFAIT PARISIENNE
CHOCOLATE MIXTURE
MELT over hot (not boiling) water
    1 6-oz. pkg. (1 c.) Semi-Sweet Chocolate Morsels
Remove from water
COMBINE and beat slightly
    2 egg yolks
    1/3 c. water
ADD slowly, beating rapidly
    Melted semi-sweet
BEAT till stiff but not dry
    2 egg whites
BEAT in gradually till stiff and glossy
    1/4 c. firmly packed brown sugar
FOLD in
    Semi-sweet mixture
    1 tsp. vanilla

WHIPPED CREAM MIXTURE
COMBINE and beat till stiff
    1 c. heavy cream
    2 tbs. brown sugar
    1 tsp. vanilla
DROP by spoonfuls in 6 to 8 5-oz. custard cups
    Chocolate Mixture
        alternately with
    Whipped Cream Mixture
Chill

YIELD: 6 to 8 servings

STACKMORES
SPREAD 6 graham crackers with
    1 tbs. marshmallow cream, each
SPRINKLE each with
    1 tsp. Semi-Sweet Chocolate Morsels
Repeat layer on each and top with graham cracker

YIELD: 6

(See illustration 27)

INSTANT PUDDING PARFAIT
PREPARE according to label directions
    1 pkg. instant vanilla or butterscotch pudding mix
COMBINE and beat till stiff
    1/2 c. heavy cream
    1/4 c. sugar
    1 tsp. Nescafé
Spoon pudding alternately with Nescafé mixture in 6 parfait glasses. Chill

REVEL PUDDINGS
COOK according to label directions
    1 pkg. vanilla pudding mix
Cool
FOLD in gently
    1/2 c. heavy cream, whipped
SPOON into parfait or sherbet glasses
    Pudding mixture
        alternately with
    Strawberry Sauce *(see page 132)*
Chill

YIELD: 6 servings

page 110 | *desserts*

BUTTERSCOTCH APPLE CRISP

Preheat oven to 375°F.

APPLE MIXTURE

SIFT together and set aside
  ½ c. sugar
  ¼ c. sifted flour
  ¼ tsp. cinnamon

PREPARE
  5 c. thinly sliced apples

ADD and mix till apples are well coated
  Sugar mixture

Turn into greased 8″ square pan

BAKE at: 375°F.

TIME: approx. 15 min.

TOPPING

MELT over hot (not boiling) water
  1 6-oz. pkg. (1 c.) Nestlé's
    Butterscotch Morsels

Remove from water

STIR in, till blended
  ¼ c. soft butter

ADD and mix with fork, till **crumbly**
  ¾ c. sifted flour
  ⅛ tsp. salt

SPRINKLE over
  Hot Apple Mixture

Return to oven

BAKE at: 375°F.

TIME: 30 min.

Serve warm with plain or whipped cream, if desired

YIELD: 8 servings

CHOCOLATE CREAM CUPS

Have ready 12 dessert shells

COMBINE in saucepan
  ½ lb. (32) marshmallows
  ⅓ c. water
  ¼ tsp. salt

Cook over moderate heat, stirring constantly, till marshmallows melt and mixture comes just to the boil

Remove from heat

ADD and stir till melted and smooth
  1 6-oz. pkg. (1 c.) Semi-Sweet
    Chocolate Morsels

FOLD into ½ c. of the semi-sweet mixture
  1 c. heavy cream, whipped
  ⅛ tsp. almond extract

Chill while preparing dessert shells

COAT sides and rims of dessert shells with
  Remaining semi-sweet mixture

ROLL coated dessert shells in
  1¼ c. finely chopped nuts

FILL prepared dessert shells with
  Chilled semi-sweet mixture

Serve immediately or chill

YIELD: 12 servings

POTS DE CREME

COMBINE and beat till thick
- 1 egg
- 2 tbs. sugar
- ⅛ tsp. salt

ADD
- ¾ c. milk

Cook over boiling water 5 min. stirring constantly

Remove from water

STIR in till smooth
- 1 6-oz. pkg. (1 c.) Semi-Sweet Chocolate Morsels
- 1 tsp. vanilla

Pour in 6 demitasse or Pot de Crème cups

Chill several hours

YIELD: 6 servings
(See illustration 19)

CHOCOLATE PUDDIN' CAKE

Have ready 2 c. 1" cake cubes

MELT over hot (not boiling) water
- 1 6-oz. pkg. (1 c.) Semi-Sweet Chocolate Morsels

Remove from water

ADD and beat well
- 1 c. cream-style cottage cheese
- 2 egg yolks
- 1 tsp. vanilla
- ⅛ tsp. almond extract
- Dash salt

BEAT till stiff but not dry
- 2 egg whites

BEAT in gradually till stiff and glossy
- ½ c. sugar

FOLD in
- Semi-sweet mixture

Cook, covered, over boiling water for 10 min.

FOLD in gently
- Cake cubes

Re-cover and cook 10 min. longer

Spoon into sherbet glasses

Serve warm or cold with ice cream or milk

YIELD: 6 servings

MINTED FLOAT

BEAT together
- 3 egg yolks
- 1 c. milk

Cook over boiling water 5 min., stirring constantly

Remove from water

STIR in till melted
- 1 6-oz. pkg. (1 c.) Semi-Sweet Chocolate Morsels

COMBINE and beat till stiff but not dry
- 3 egg whites
- 1 tsp. vanilla
- ⅛ to ¼ tsp. peppermint extract

BEAT in gradually till stiff and glossy
- ½ c. sugar

FOLD in
- Semi-sweet mixture

Pour in 8 sherbet glasses

Chill

To serve: Decorate with shredded coconut or slivered almonds

YIELD: 8 servings

CROQUEMBOUCHE

Preheat oven to 425°F.

PREPARE according to pkg. directions
 1 pkg. cream puff mix

Place on 8″ circle of waxed paper or ungreased cookie sheet

SPREAD over waxed paper to cover
 3 tbs. batter

Prick well with fork

DROP 12 mounds around edge of circle, using
 1 level tsp. batter for each

Drop remaining batter, by level tea-spoons, 2″ apart on ungreased cookie sheet

BAKE at: 425°F.

TIME: approx. 20 min.

Remove from oven, cut slits in sides of puffs. Return to oven for 5 min. to dry out

Cool. Remove waxed paper; place on serving plate

Prepare

SYRUP GLAZE

COMBINE and bring to boil over mod-erate heat, stirring constantly
 1 c. light corn syrup
 1 c. sugar
 1 tbs. Nescafé
 1 tbs. water

Boil 5 min. over moderate heat, stirring constantly

Cool to lukewarm

Prepare

FILLING

COMBINE and bring to boil, stirring constantly
 ½ c. light corn syrup
 2 tbs. water
 ⅛ tsp. salt

Remove from heat

ADD and stir till melted
 1 6-oz. pkg. (1 c.) Semi-Sweet
 Chocolate Morsels

ADD
 2 tbs. bourbon

FOLD in
 1 c. heavy cream, whipped

TO ASSEMBLE

FILL individual puffs and those around edge of circle with
 Filling

DRIZZLE slowly over circle
 2 tbs. warm* Syrup Glaze

Place 7 or 8 filled puffs in center of circle and again drizzle with Syrup Glaze

Top with approx. 12 filled puffs and again drizzle with Syrup Glaze

Continue to build in layers, drizz-ling each with Syrup Glaze, to form a pyramid

Chill 4 to 6 hours

Chill or freeze remaining filled puffs for later use

*Reheat Syrup Glaze over hot water, if necessary.

YIELD: 25 servings
(See illustration 17)

15 Every dinner party deserves a show-stopper—and yours can be this light-as-a-cloud Bain Marie Soufflé Chocolat (p. 125). Let guests sample it as it is, or spoon tasty Apricot Fluff over each portion.

16 Two dramatic creations. Treat family and guests to the refreshing flavor of Bavarian Mint Pie (p. 97) with its unusual chocolate-nut crust, or the Butterscotch Pecan Pie (p. 94), reminiscent of the Old South.

17 French-inspired and elegant, this Croquembouche (p. 112) is a marvelous pyramid glistening with a rich syrup glaze. It makes an unusual, *trés différent* dessert for company.

18 Here's a pretty piece of pastry that deserves an honored place on your table. It's Mocha Angel Pie (p. 90), ringed with puffs of whipped cream. It's sure to win plaudits time and again from lucky guests.

19 For the variety that is the spice of life, serve guests these thimble-sized delicacies: *(clockwise from lower left)* Petit Puff Café (p. 105), Mousse Au Chocolat (p. 123), "Laced" Chocolate Bavarian (p. 107), Pot de Crème (p. 111), Chocolate Charlotte Russe (p. 106), Nescafé Tortoni (p. 149), Napoleonette (p. 108).

20 The tantalizing Frozen Cream Chiffon Roll (p. 150) makes a patriotic dessert when you decorate it — as shown here — with George Washington's famous hatchet and cherries. Its beverage partner: a steaming mug of hot chocolate topped with fluffy whipped cream.

21 For perfect picnics, pack a basket of Irish Whirligigs (p. 68) and a fresh-from-the-kitchen Hawaiian Pineapple Cake (p. 18). A real thirst-quencher is Honeyed Orange Cooler (p. 179). Accompany with Swiss Knight Process Gruyère Cheese, crackers and apples.

15

16

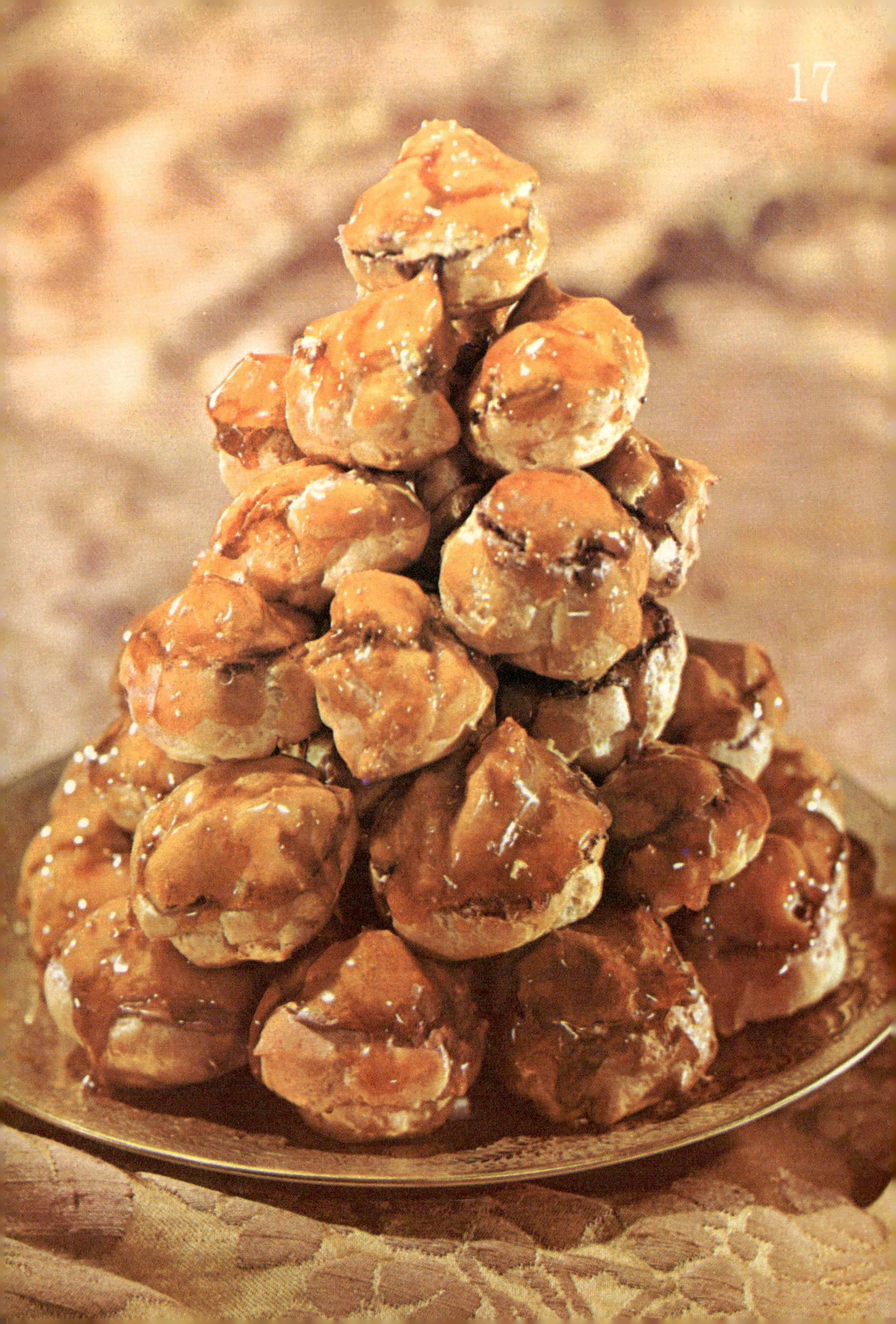
17

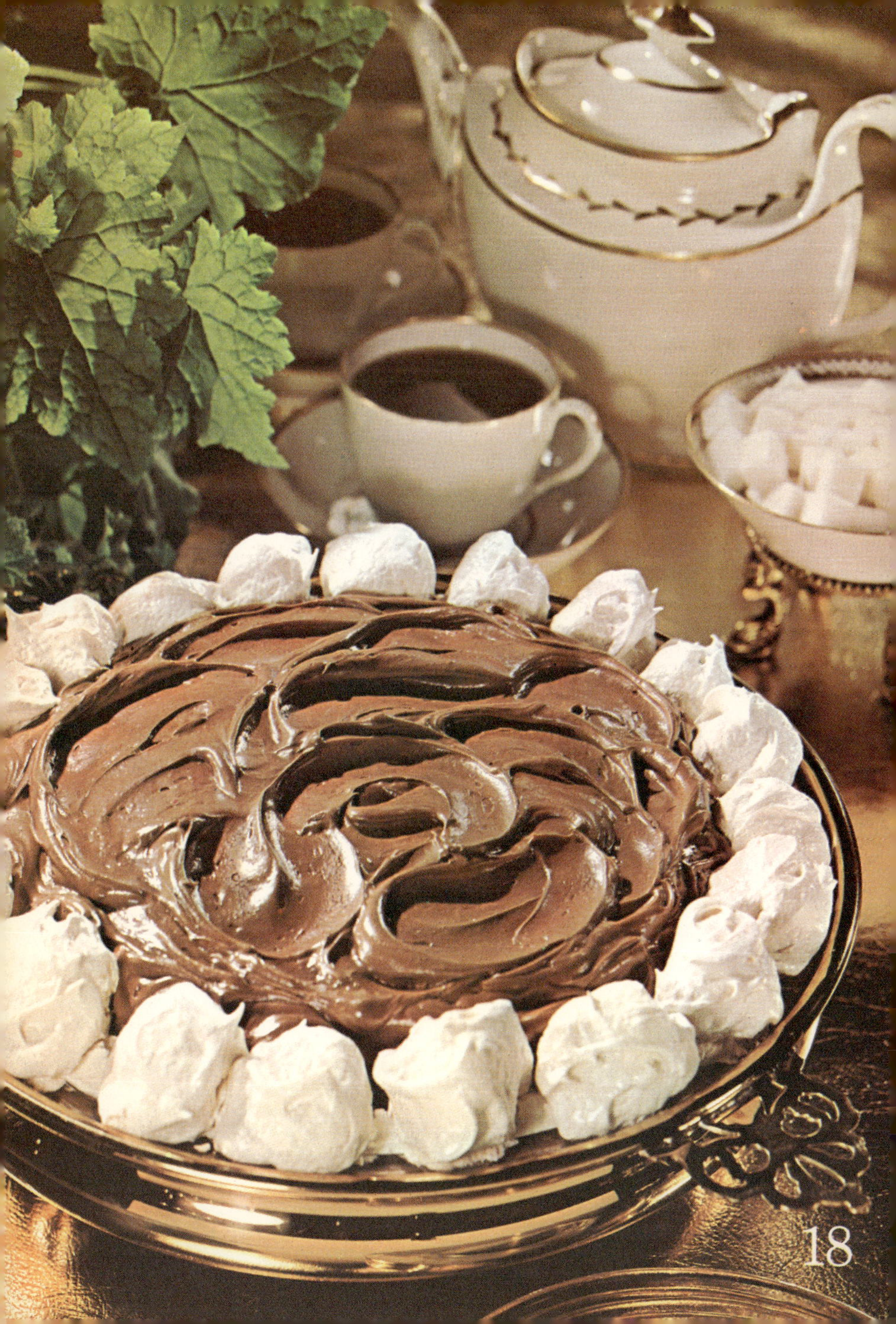

19

20

21

MOCHA BAVARIAN

COMBINE in saucepan and cook over moderate heat till gelatin dissolves and mixture *just* comes to boil, stirring constantly
- ½ c. milk
- ¼ c. sugar
- 1 tbs. Nescafé
- 1 envelope unflavored gelatin

Remove from heat

BEAT slightly
- 2 egg yolks

ADD gradually, stirring rapidly
- Nescafé mixture

Cook over moderate heat 2 min., stirring constantly

Remove from heat

STIR in till melted
- 1 6-oz. pkg. (1 c.) Semi-Sweet Chocolate Morsels

BLEND in
- ½ c. milk
- 2 tbs. brandy

Chill till thickened but not set

BEAT till stiff but not dry
- 2 egg whites

BEAT in gradually till stiff and glossy
- ½ c. sugar

FOLD in
- Semi-sweet mixture
- ½ c. heavy cream, whipped

Chill till thickened, but not set

Spoon into 8 to 10 sherbet glasses

Chill

YIELD: 8 to 10 servings

PARTY CHOCOLATE CHEESE CAKE

Preheat oven to 325°F.

SIFT together and set aside
- 1 c. sifted flour
- ¼ c. sugar
- ¼ tsp. salt

BLEND in till crumbly
- ⅓ c. butter

Press into bottom of 9" springform pan

BAKE at: 325°F.

TIME: 15 to 20 min.

MELT over hot (not boiling) water
- 1 6-oz. pkg. (1 c.) Semi-Sweet Chocolate Morsels

Remove from heat

BLEND in
- 1 8-oz. pkg. cream cheese

BEAT in
- 2 eggs

STIR in
- ¾ c. sugar
- 2 tbs. flour
- ¼ tsp. salt

BLEND in thoroughly
- 1 c. sour cream
- 1 tsp. vanilla

BAKE at: 325°F.

TIME: approx. 1 hr. 30 min., or till set in the center

YIELD: 10 to 12 servings

page 122 / desserts

Subtle Soufflés, Mousses and Tortes

DELICATE CHOCOLATE SOUFFLÉ CUPS

Preheat oven to 325°F.

MELT over hot (not boiling) water
1 6-oz. pkg. (1 c.) Semi-Sweet Chocolate Morsels
2 tbs. butter

STIR in till well blended
¼ c. flour
½ tsp. salt

COMBINE and add gradually
1 c. milk
1½ tsp. vanilla

Cook over low heat, stirring constantly, till thickened

BEAT till thick
3 egg yolks

BEAT in gradually till light
⅓ c. sugar

STIR into beaten egg yolk mixture
Semi-sweet mixture

BEAT till stiff but not dry
3 egg whites

FOLD into
Semi-sweet mixture

Spoon into 10 buttered 6-oz. custard cups

Place in shallow baking pan. Fill pan with water to depth of 1"

BAKE at: 325°F.

TIME: 40 to 45 min.

Serve hot with whipped cream, if desired

YIELD: 10 servings

CHOCOLATE HEAVENLY CROWN

Have ready 18 ladyfingers, split lengthwise. Place cut side down in 375°F. oven for 5 min. Cool approx. 10 min.

BRUSH cut sides with
½ c. orange juice

Place approx. 22 pieces vertically around edge of lightly buttered 9" springform pan. Arrange remaining pieces on bottom of pan. Set aside

FILLING

MELT over hot (not boiling) water
1 6-oz. pkg. (1 c.) Semi-Sweet Chocolate Morsels

Remove from water

Cool approx. 10 min.

BLEND
½ lb. cream cheese, softened
½ c. firmly packed brown sugar
⅛ tsp. salt

BEAT in one at a time
3 egg yolks

STIR in
Cooled semi-sweet

COMBINE and beat till stiff but not dry
3 egg whites
1½ tsp. vanilla

BEAT gradually till stiff and satiny
½ c. firmly packed brown sugar

FOLD into semi-sweet mixture
1½ c. heavy cream, whipped
Egg white mixture

Pour into ladyfinger-lined springform pan

Chill at least 5 hrs. or overnight

YIELD: approx. 12 servings

MOCHA NUT TORTE

Preheat oven to 300°F.

MERINGUE CIRCLES

COMBINE and beat till stiff but not dry
- 3 egg whites
- ¼ tsp. salt
- ½ tsp. almond extract

BEAT in gradually till stiff and satiny
- ¾ c. light brown sugar, firmly packed

FOLD in
- ½ c. nuts, finely chopped

Spread on four 8" circles cut from brown paper. Place on ungreased cookie sheets

COMBINE
- 1 tsp. Nescafé
- 3 tbs. light brown sugar

Sprinkle Nescafé mixture in 1" border around edge of *one* circle only

BAKE at 300°F. 35 min.

Cool. Peel off paper gently

FILLING

COMBINE and melt over moderate heat, stirring constantly
- ¼ lb. (16) marshmallows
- ⅓ c. water
- ⅛ tsp. salt
- 1 tbs. Nescafé

BEAT well
- 3 egg yolks

ADD slowly, stirring rapidly
- Nescafé mixture

Cook over moderate heat 1 min., stirring constantly

Remove from heat

STIR in till melted
- 1 6-oz. pkg. (1 c.) Semi-Sweet Chocolate Morsels

Cool approx. 5 min.

FOLD in
- ½ c. heavy cream, whipped
- 1 tsp. vanilla

Chill till thick enough to spread

Spread over three meringue circles. Place one above the other, topping with decorated circle. Frost sides with Nescafé Cream

NESCAFÉ CREAM

COMBINE and beat till stiff
- ½ c. heavy cream
- 1 tbs. Nescafé
- ¼ c. light brown sugar, firmly packed
- ⅛ tsp. almond extract

Chill several hours or overnight

YIELD: 10 servings

MOUSSE AU CHOCOLAT

MELT over hot (not boiling) water
- 1 6-oz. pkg. Semi-Sweet Chocolate Morsels

Remove from heat

ADD
- 6 egg yolks, slightly beaten with
- 2 tbs. cognac

BEAT till stiff but not dry
- 6 egg whites
- Dash salt

Fold gently into chocolate mixture. Pour into sherbet glasses. Chill. Serve with plain cream

YIELD: 8 servings

(See illustration 19)

NEW ORLEANS TORTE

Preheat oven to 300°F.

MERINGUE CIRCLES

BEAT till blended and foamy
  3 egg whites
  ½ tsp. almond extract
  ¼ tsp. salt

BEAT in gradually till stiff,
glossy peaks form
  ¾ c. firmly packed brown sugar

FOLD in
  ½ c. finely chopped nuts

Spread on four 8″ circles cut from
brown paper. Sprinkle top of one
circle with
  1 tsp. colored sugar or multi-
    colored nonpareils

Place on ungreased cookie sheets

BAKE at: 300° F.

TIME: 35 min.

Cool. Peel off paper gently

FILLING-FROSTING

MELT over hot (not boiling) water
  1 6-oz. pkg. (1 c.) Semi-Sweet
    Chocolate Morsels

Cool approx. 10 min.

BEAT till creamy
  1 8-oz. pkg. cream cheese

BLEND in
  1 tbs. milk

BEAT in gradually
  ¾ c. firmly packed brown sugar
  ⅛ tsp. salt

FOLD into cooled semi-sweet
  Cream cheese mixture
  1 c. heavy cream, whipped
  1 tsp. vanilla

Spread ¾ c. Filling-Frosting on 3
plain meringue circles. Stack in layers. Top with trimmed circle. Cover
sides and 1″ around edge of top
circle with remaining Filling-Frosting

Chill for several hours or overnight

Cut in wedges to serve

  YIELD: 12 to 16 servings
  (See illustration 2)

MOUSSE CHOCOLAT DE BRAZIL

MELT over hot (not boiling) water
  1 6-oz. pkg. (1 c.) Semi-Sweet
    Chocolate Morsels

BEAT in, one at a time
  4 egg yolks

Remove from water

BLEND in
  1 tsp. Nescafé
  ½ tsp. rum extract

BEAT till blended and foamy
  4 egg whites
  Dash of salt

ADD gradually and continue beating
till stiff and glossy
  ½ c. sugar

FOLD in
  Semi-sweet mixture

Spoon into five or six 5-oz.
custard cups

Chill. Serve garnished with whipped
cream, if desired

  YIELD: 5 to 6 servings

BAIN MARIE SOUFFLÉ CHOCOLAT

MELT over hot (not boiling) water
- 1 6-oz. pkg. (1 c.) Semi-Sweet Chocolate Morsels

Remove from water

COMBINE and beat till blended and foamy
- 4 egg whites
- ¼ tsp. salt
- ¼ tsp. cream of tartar

BEAT in gradually till stiff, glossy peaks form
- ¼ c. firmly packed brown sugar

FOLD in
- Melted semi-sweet

Pour in top of buttered 2-qt. double boiler. Cook, covered, over boiling water for 1 hr. and 20 min.

Serve with

APRICOT FLUFF

COMBINE in small mixing bowl and beat at high speed till thick and fluffy
- 1 c. well-drained, canned, apricot halves, sieved
- ½ c. sugar
- 1 egg white
- Dash salt

YIELD: 5 to 6 servings
(See illustration 15)

BROWN ORCHID SOUFFLÉ

Preheat oven to 325°F.

COMBINE in saucepan
- ¾ c. sugar
- ½ c. sifted flour
- ¾ tsp. salt

COMBINE and stir in gradually
- 1⅓ c. milk
- 1 tsp. vanilla

Cook, stirring constantly over medium heat, till thickened

Reserve ⅔ c. of mixture

STIR into remainder in saucepan
- 1 6-oz. pkg. (1 c.) Semi-Sweet Chocolate Morsels

BEAT till thick
- 6 egg yolks

COMBINE and beat till stiff but not dry
- 6 egg whites
- ¼ tsp. cream of tartar

FOLD into reserved sauce mixture
- ½ of beaten egg yolks
- ½ of egg white mixture

FOLD into semi-sweet mixture
- Remaining egg yolks
- Remaining egg white mixture

Spoon the two mixtures alternately into ungreased 2-qt. casserole

BAKE at: 325°F.

TIME: 65 to 75 min.

Serve immediately topped with ice cream, if desired

YIELD: 8 to 10 servings

SOUFFLÉ AU CHOCOLAT FROID

COMBINE in top of double boiler and cook over hot water, stirring till gelatin is dissolved and chocolate is melted

    1 6-oz. pkg. (1 c.) Semi-Sweet
        Chocolate Morsels
    ¼ c. water
    1 envelope unflavored gelatin
    ½ c. firmly packed brown sugar

STIR in and beat till light

    4 egg yolks
    ⅓ c. orange juice or fruit-
        flavored liqueur

Remove from water

BEAT till stiff but not dry

    4 egg whites
    ¼ tsp. salt

BEAT in gradually till glossy peaks form

    ½ c. firmly packed brown sugar

FOLD in

    Semi-sweet mixture
    1 c. heavy cream, whipped

Pour mixture into foil-lined 9″ square pan*. Chill till firm—several hours or overnight

Lift from pan. Peel foil from sides and cut in approx. 2″ squares. Place each square on serving dish

Prepare

CHOCOLATE LEAF

COMBINE and melt over hot (not boiling) water

    1 6-oz. pkg. (1 c.) Semi-Sweet
        Chocolate Morsels
    1 tbs. shortening

Spread evenly on waxed paper-lined cookie sheet to rectangle 15″ x 12″. Chill till firm. Invert on waxed

paper. Gently peel off waxed paper. Cut with sharp knife into oblongs 2″ x 1½″

Press a Chocolate Leaf oblong onto each side of each square of
    Chocolate Soufflé mixture

Decorate with whipped cream

Chill till ready to serve

YIELD: 16 servings

*Allow foil to come up above top of pan, for easy removal

Dessert Pancakes, Waffles, Doughnuts

CHOCOLATE DESSERT PANCAKES

COMBINE and stir briskly

    1 c. Nestlé's Chocolate Quik
    ½ c. milk

STIR in

    2 beaten eggs
    ¼ c. melted shortening
    ¾ tsp. vanilla

ADD and mix *just* till blended

    1 c. pancake mix
    ⅓ c. sugar

POUR on lightly greased griddle using

    ¼ c. batter for each

Bake according to package directions

YIELD: approx. 6 pancakes

CHOCOLATE DESSERT WAFFLES

COMBINE and melt over hot (not boiling) water
- 1 6-oz. pkg. (1 c.) Semi-Sweet Chocolate Morsels
- ⅓ c. shortening

Remove from heat

SIFT together and set aside
- 1 c. sifted flour
- 1 tsp. baking soda
- ¼ tsp. salt

BEAT till thick and lemon-colored
- 2 eggs

ADD gradually and beat till *very* thick
- ½ c. sugar

STIR in and blend well
- Flour mixture alternately with
- ½ c. milk

ADD
- Semi-sweet mixture

Bake in waffle iron as manufacturer directs

YIELD: approx. 4 waffles

TWO-TONE DOUGHNUT CRUMBLE

COMBINE and mix well
- 1 19-oz. can crushed pineapple, drained
- 4 doughnuts, crumbled

Divide into 6 sherbet glasses

SAUCE

Prepare Dark Magic Sauce *(see page 131)*

Fill sherbet dishes with Dark Magic Sauce

Chill

YIELD: 6 servings

DOUGHNUT MERINGUE CUPS

Preheat oven to 325°F.

PRESS into four 5-oz. custard cups
- 4 doughnuts

DRAIN, reserving 4 tbs. syrup
- 1 1-lb. can sliced peaches

POUR over *each* doughnut
- 1 tbs. reserved syrup

PLACE over *each* doughnut
- ¼ of drained peaches
- and sprinkle with
- 2 tbs. Semi-Sweet Chocolate Morsels

Prepare

MERINGUE

BEAT till foamy
- 1 egg white

ADD gradually and continue beating till stiff, glossy peaks form
- 2 tbs. sugar

Spread over peaches and chocolate morsels

BAKE at: 325°F.
TIME: 18 min.

YIELD: 4 servings

page 128 / desserts

DOUGHNUT DESSERT LOG

CUT in half, crosswise
  12 doughnuts, coated with
    confectioners' sugar

BRUSH cut sides with
  Milk or orange juice
    (approx. ¾ c.)

MELT over hot (not boiling) water
  1 6-oz. pkg. (1 c.) Semi-Sweet
    Chocolate Morsels

Remove from water

Cool approx. 10 min.

COMBINE and blend well
  1 8-oz. pkg. cottage cheese
  ½ c. firmly packed brown sugar

STIR in
  Melted semi-sweet

FOLD in
  1 c. heavy cream, whipped

Spread about ⅔ of the semi-sweet mixture on cut surfaces of doughnuts

Place 12 doughnut halves together to make a log. Repeat for second log

Press ends of "logs" together to seal

Frost ends and sides (not tops) with remaining semi-sweet mixture

Chill several hours or overnight

To serve: Cut on the diagonal in ½" slices

  YIELD: approx. 24 servings

STRAWBERRY DESSERT PANCAKES

COMBINE and stir briskly
  ¾ c. milk
  ⅓ c. Nestlé's Strawberry Quik

STIR in
  2 beaten eggs
  ¼ c. melted shortening
  ¼ tsp. lemon extract

ADD and mix *just* till moistened
  1¼ c. pancake mix
  ⅓ c. sugar

POUR on lightly greased griddle for each pancake
  ¼ c. batter

Bake according to package directions

  YIELD: approx. 12 pancakes

Saucy Sauces and Tempting Toppings

1, 2, 3 SAUCE

MIX till well blended
  ½ c. Nestlé's Chocolate Quik
  1 tbs. boiling water

STIR in
  ¼ c. corn syrup

Serve on ice cream or desserts, or as glaze on cakes or pastries

  YIELD: approx. ½ c.

CHOCOLATE-PEANUT SAUCE

MELT over hot (not boiling) water
- 1 6-oz. pkg. (1 c.) Semi-Sweet Chocolate Morsels
- ½ c. peanut butter

BLEND in
- ¾ c. milk

Serve warm over ice cream or cake

YIELD: 1¾ c.

(See illustration 25)

CANDIED FRUIT TOPPING

MELT over hot (not boiling) water
- 1 6-oz. pkg. (1 c.) Semi-Sweet Chocolate Morsels

Remove from water

COMBINE
- ½ c. mixed candied fruit, coarsely chopped
- ¼ c. water

STIR in
- Melted semi-sweet
- ¼ tsp. rum extract (optional)

Serve warm or cool over ice cream or cake

YIELD: approx. 1 c.

HONEY PEANUT BUTTER TOPPING

COMBINE and melt over hot (not boiling) water
- 1 6-oz. pkg. (1 c.) Semi-Sweet Chocolate Morsels
- ¼ c. honey
- ¼ c. water
- 2 tbs. peanut butter

Serve warm or cool over ice cream or cake

YIELD: approx. 1⅛ c.

ORANGE MARMALADE TOPPING

COMBINE and melt over hot (not boiling) water
- 1 6-oz. pkg. (1 c.) Semi-Sweet Chocolate Morsels
- ⅓ c. hot water

STIR in
- ⅓ c. orange marmalade

Serve warm or cool over ice cream or cake

YIELD: approx. 1⅛ c.

PINEAPPLE BUTTERSCOTCH SAUCE

COMBINE in a saucepan, and bring *just* to a boil
- 1 c. drained, crushed pineapple
- ½ c. light corn syrup

Remove from heat

ADD at once and stir till blended and smooth
- 1 6-oz. pkg. (1 c.) Butterscotch Morsels

Serve warm over ice cream or warm cake

YIELD: approx. 2 c.

desserts

page 130 / desserts

CREAMY CHOCOLATE SAUCE

COMBINE in small saucepan and bring *just* to boil over moderate heat, stirring constantly

¼ c. honey

1 tbs. water

Remove from heat

ADD and stir till blended and smooth

1 6-oz. pkg. (1 c.) Semi-Sweet Chocolate Morsels

1 tsp. vanilla

Cool about 10 min.

FOLD in

1 c. heavy cream, whipped

BLEND in gradually

⅓ c. water

Serve over ice cream or warm cake at once OR chill before serving

YIELD: approx. 3 cups

SPEEDY FUDGE SAUCE

MELT over hot (not boiling) water

1 6-oz. pkg. (1 c.) Semi-Sweet Chocolate Morsels

ADD and stir till smooth

⅓ c. sweetened condensed milk

⅓ c. water

1 tsp. vanilla

Serve warm*

YIELD: approx. 1 c.

Variations: Add while warm, one of the following:

1. 1 tsp. Nescafé
2. ¼ c. marshmallow cream
3. ¼ c. peanut butter
4. ½ c. shredded or toasted coconut
5. ½ c. salted peanuts

*After standing, sauces may be thinned by adding a small amount of boiling water

OLYMPIA CHOCOLATE SAUCE

COMBINE in small, heavy saucepan and bring to boil over moderate heat stirring constantly

1 14-oz. can (1¼ c.) sweetened condensed milk

¼ c. butter

¼ tsp. salt

Boil 1 min., stirring constantly

Remove from heat

ADD and stir till blended and smooth

1 6-oz. pkg. (1 c.) Semi-Sweet Chocolate Morsels

1 tsp. vanilla

STIR in gradually

¼ c. water

Serve over ice cream or warm cake

YIELD: approx. 2 c.

Note: Sauce may be reheated over very low heat

DARK MAGIC SAUCE

MELT over hot (not boiling) water
  1 6-oz. pkg. (1 c.) Semi-Sweet Chocolate Morsels

ADD and stir to blend thoroughly
  1 c. commercial sour cream
  1 tbs. water
  ¼ tsp. salt

FOLD in
  1 c. miniature marshmallows

YIELD: 2½ c.

CHOCOLATE MARSHMALLOW SAUCE

COMBINE and bring *just* to boil over moderate heat, stirring constantly
  ½ c. milk
  ¼ c. butter or margarine
  ⅛ tsp. salt

Remove from heat

ADD and stir till blended and smooth
  1 6-oz. pkg. (1 c.) Semi-Sweet Chocolate Morsels
  1 tsp. vanilla

BEAT in gradually
  1 7½-oz. jar marshmallow cream

Serve over ice cream or cake

YIELD: 2¼ c.

(See illustration 25)

HOT FUDGE SAUCE

COMBINE in saucepan and bring *just* to boil, over moderate heat, stirring constantly
  ½ c. corn syrup
  ½ c. light cream
  ¼ c. sugar
  1 tbs. water

Remove from heat

ADD and stir till melted and smooth
  1 6-oz. pkg. (1 c.) Semi-Sweet Chocolate Morsels

BLEND in
  1 tsp. vanilla

Serve hot

YIELD: 8 servings

COFFEE HARD SAUCE

COMBINE and beat till light
  ⅓ c. soft butter
  1 tbs. cream
  1 tsp. Nescafé

BEAT in gradually
  1 c. sifted confectioners' sugar

Chill

Serve with hot apple pie, apple dumpling, Brown Betty, or plum pudding

YIELD: approx. 1 c.

page 132 / desserts

CHOCOLATE DIPS

MELT over hot (not boiling) water
   1 6-oz. pkg. (1 c.) Semi-Sweet
      Chocolate Morsels

BLEND in
   1 1-lb. can whole cranberry sauce
   2 tbs. sugar

Use as dip for pretzels, crackers or
potato chips

YIELD: 2½ c.

Variations: Substitute for cranberry sauce and sugar

1. 1 c. drained, cooked or canned
   apricots, sieved
2. 3 bananas, finely mashed
   ½ c. chunk-style peanut butter
   Dash salt
3. 1 c. marmalade
4. 1 7½-oz. jar marshmallow
   cream
   1 c. drained crushed pineapple

STRAWBERRY SAUCE

COMBINE in 1-qt. saucepan; bring to
a full rolling boil over high heat,
stirring constantly
   1 c. Nestlé's Strawberry Quik
   ¼ c. corn syrup
   ¼ c. water
   1 tbs. lemon juice

Remove from heat. Chill

Use as sauce on ice cream, custard,
fruits, and puddings

YIELD: approx. ¾ c.

(See illustration 25)

STRAWBERRY WHIPPED CREAM

PLACE in bowl and chill
   1 c. heavy cream
   ¼ c. Nestlé's Strawberry Quik
   Dash salt

Beat till thick

Use as cake frosting* or as topping
on desserts

YIELD: 2 c.

*When used as cake frosting, chill
before serving

BUTTERSCOTCH SAUCE

COMBINE; bring *just* to boil over
moderate heat, stirring constantly
   ¼ c. light corn syrup
   ¼ c. evaporated milk

Remove from heat

STIR in till smooth
   1 6-oz. pkg. (1 c.)
      Butterscotch Morsels

Serve warm over ice cream or
warm cake

YIELD: 1 c.

Note: If sauce becomes too thick on
standing, reheat over hot water

SOUR CREAM TOPPING

MELT over hot (not boiling) water
   1 6-oz. pkg. (1 c.) Semi-Sweet Chocolate Morsels

Remove from water

BLEND in
   ½ c. sour cream
   ½ tsp. cinnamon
   ⅛ tsp. salt

STIR in
   ¼ c. water or milk

Serve over individual cake portions

YIELD: approx. 1¼ c.

PANCAKE NESCAFÉ SAUCE

COMBINE
   ½ c. sugar
   1 tbs. cornstarch
   1 tsp. Nescafé
   ⅛ tsp. salt

ADD and stir gradually till smooth
   1 c. water

Bring to a full boil, over moderate heat, stirring constantly

Cook 3 min., stirring constantly

ADD
   1 tbs. butter

Serve hot over pancakes or waffles

YIELD: 1¼ c.

CHOCOLATE QUIK SAUCE

MIX till well blended
   1 c. Nestlé's Chocolate Quik
   2 tbs. water

ADD and bring *just* to boil over moderate heat, stirring constantly
   ⅓ c. sweetened condensed milk

Serve warm over ice cream or cake

YIELD: approx. ¾ c.

Commercial doughnuts become festive additions to the breakfast, luncheon, or dinner table, when you decorate them with any of our delicious toppings. Try a do-it-yourself-doughnut Lazy Susan at your next bridge party. Just line up attractive matching bowls with one pineapple-butterscotch, one chocolate, one coffee topping—and as many more as you, and your guests, may dare. The same idea will make a hit when your youngsters descend on you with four or five little friends —all with big appetites.

Candy— Sweets for the Sweet

"Sugar 'n' Spice 'n' everything nice"—that's what this chapter is made of.

Candies to brighten up the day—any day—are to be found here! Traditional candies for holidays, for parties, for the family's sweet tooth. A special section is devoted to Christmas, including some eye-catching suggestions for wrappings that will dress your lovingly-made gifts in the packages they deserve.

No dessert cook book could overlook that most nostalgic of all sweets —fudge. Fudge of many varieties are here for your young ones to learn, and for you to discover anew. For many of us, fudge was the object of our first cooking efforts, and who doesn't remember the pleasures of bowl-and-spoon-lickin'? Even if you learned how to make fudge 'way back for your first "grown up" party, here are some new, quick twists on this old family delight. There are not many who can resist the fragrance of home kitchen-made fudge, and whether he's two or seventy-two, there are few quicker ways to a man's heart.

We haven't neglected the many other sweet favorites, either. There are crunchy fruit crisps, toffee which melts on your tongue, pralines to remind you of New Orleans, butterscotch apples, nut-filled caramels, and a few original recipes to start your reputation blooming as one who knows her way around the kitchen. Our improved kitchen-tested techniques and recipes are so foolproof that you won't even need that old fashioned candy thermometer.

Candy you've made in your own kitchen has so much more meaning, somehow, than candy you've purchased. The recipient is sure to know how warmly your gift is offered, since so much of you went into the making of it.

Everyone's Favorite —Fudge

SHORT CUT FUDGE

MELT over hot (not boiling) water
>2 6-oz. pkgs. or 1 12-oz. pkg. (2 c.) Nestlé's Semi-Sweet Chocolate Morsels

Remove from water

ADD and stir in till smooth and satiny—*do not beat*
>⅔ c. sweetened condensed milk
>1 tbs. water
>1 tsp. vanilla

Spread in greased pan 10″ x 5″ x 3″ or drop by teaspoonfuls on waxed paper-lined cookie sheet

Chill till firm

>**YIELD:** approx. 1¼ lbs.

Variations:

1. FUDGE BALLS: Chill till firm enough to handle. Form in small balls. Roll in: Nestlé's EverReady Cocoa, Nestlé's Chocolate Quik, coconut, chopped nuts, candied fruit, almond slivers

2. FUDGE LOGS OR CRESCENTS: Form into small finger-like logs. For crescents, shape logs to form horseshoes. Dip ends in melted semi-sweet, then in finely chopped nuts. Chill on waxed paper

3. VARIETY DROPS: Add *one* of the following with the condensed milk mixture
>¼ c. peanut butter
>>*and* 1 additional tbs. water

>1½ c. nuts, coarsely chopped,
>>*and* ½ c. raisins

>1 tbs. Nescafé (substitute ¼ tsp. almond extract for vanilla)
>1¼ c. (½ lb.) small gumdrops

>**YIELD:** 4 to 5 dozen drops

(See illustration 10)

EASY CREAMY FUDGE

MELT over hot (not boiling) water
>1 6-oz. pkg. (1 c.) Semi-Sweet Chocolate Morsels
>1 3-oz. pkg. cream cheese

Remove from heat

BLEND in
>¼ c. sifted confectioners' sugar
>¼ c. honey
>½ tsp. vanilla
>⅛ tsp. salt

ADD and mix well
>2 c. finely crushed vanilla wafers (approx. 40 small wafers)
>½ c. chopped walnuts

Form* into 1″ balls, using 1 level tablespoon for each. Roll in finely chopped nuts, if desired, or press walnut half into tops to make patties

Chill till firm

>**YIELD:** approx. 3 dozen

*Or press evenly into a greased or foil-lined 10″ x 5″ x 3″ pan. Chill and cut into squares

CHOCOLATE FUDGIES

COMBINE and stir till blended over hot (not boiling) water
> 2 6-oz. pkgs. or 1 12-oz. pkg. (2 c.) Semi-Sweet Chocolate Morsels
> ½ c. water
> ½ c. maple-blended syrup

COMBINE in bowl and mix well
> 3 c. finely crushed vanilla wafer crumbs
> 2 c. miniature marshmallows
> 2 c. coarsely chopped nuts
> 1 c. sifted confectioners' sugar
> ½ tsp. Nescafé
> ½ tsp. salt

RESERVE and set aside
> ½ c. semi-sweet mixture

ADD to crumb mixture and mix till well blended
> Remaining semi-sweet mixture

Press evenly into well-greased 9″ square pan

Top with

GLAZE

REPLACE over hot water
> Reserved ½ c. semi-sweet mixture

ADD and stir till melted
> 2 tsp. shortening

STIR in
> ½ c. coarsely chopped nuts

Spoon over mixture in pan, spreading to cover completely

Cool

Cut in 1″ squares

YIELD: 81 squares

QUIK FUDGIES

COMBINE in 2½-qt. bowl and mix till Quik is all moistened
> 1½ c. Nestlé's Chocolate Quik
> ¼ c. water
> ½ tsp. salt

ADD and bring *just* to boil, stirring constantly
> ½ c. maple-blended syrup

Cool approx. 10 min.

ADD and mix well
> 2 c. finely crushed vanilla wafer crumbs
> 1 c. chopped nuts

STIR in
> 2 c. miniature marshmallows

Press into greased 8″ square pan

Let stand (at room temp.) till set

Cut in 1″ squares

YIELD: 64 squares

EVERREADY CAMPERS' FUDGE

COMBINE in 8″ or 9″ square pan
> 1 1-lb. pkg. confectioners' sugar
> 1 ½-lb. tin Nestlé's EverReady Cocoa

ADD and mix with fork
> ¼ c. hot water
> 2 tbs. butter

Knead till smooth*. Pat evenly in pan and cut in squares

*If necessary add 1 to 2 tsp. hot water gradually

EASY BUTTERSCOTCH FUDGE

MELT over hot (not boiling) water
   2 6-oz. pkgs. (2 c.) Nestlé's
      Butterscotch Morsels

Remove from water

ADD and stir till smooth and satiny
—*do not beat*
   ⅔ c. sweetened condensed milk
   1 tsp. vanilla

Spread in greased 10″ x 5″ x 3″ pan or drop by teaspoonfuls on waxed paper-lined cookie sheet

Chill till firm

Variation:

BUTTERSCOTCH PECAN ROLLS: Shape fudge into two 12″ rolls. Mark surface, lengthwise, with tines of fork. Brush with slightly beaten egg white. Press pecan halves into entire surface of rolls. Wrap in waxed paper. Chill. Cut in ½″ slices, to serve

          YIELD: 4 dozen slices

BUTTERSCOTCH-PEANUT BUTTER FUDGE

COMBINE in top of double boiler
   2 6-oz. pkgs. (2 c.)
      Butterscotch Morsels
   ½ c. chunk-style peanut butter

Place over hot (not boiling) water till butterscotch melts. Stir till blended

ADD and stir *just* till blended
   ⅔ c. sweetened condensed milk

Spread in greased or foil-lined 8″ square pan

Chill till firm. Cut in squares

          YIELD: approx. 1½ lbs.

BUTTERSCOTCH CREAM FUDGE

COMBINE in saucepan and bring to *full* boil over moderate heat, stirring constantly
   1 jar marshmallow cream*
   1½ c. sugar
   ⅔ c. evaporated milk
   ¼ c. butter
   ¼ tsp. salt

Boil 5 min. over moderate heat, stirring constantly

Remove from heat

STIR in till melted
   2 6-oz. pkgs. (2 c.)
      Butterscotch Morsels

ADD
   ½ c. chopped nuts, if desired
   1 tsp. vanilla

Pour in greased 8″ square pan

Chill till firm

          YIELD: approx. 2⅓ lbs.

*5-oz. to 10-oz. jar

page 138 / candies

MARSHMALLOW CREAM FUDGE

COMBINE and bring to a *full* boil stirring constantly
- 1½ c. sugar
- 1 jar marshmallow cream*
- ⅔ c. evaporated milk
- ¼ c. butter or margarine
- ¼ tsp. salt

Boil 5 min. over moderate heat, stirring constantly

Remove from heat

STIR in till melted
- 2 6-oz. or 1 12-oz. pkg. (2 c.) Semi-Sweet Chocolate Morsels

ADD
- ½ c. chopped nuts (optional)
- 1 tsp. vanilla

Pour in greased 8″ square pan. Chill till firm

YIELD: approx. 2¼ lbs.

*5-oz. to 10-oz. jar OR substitute ½ lb. (32) large marshmallows or 2½ c. miniature marshmallows and increase evaporated milk to 1 c.
(See illustration 10)

Candy Classics

SCOTCH CRISPIES

MELT over hot (not boiling) water
- 1 6-oz. pkg. (1 c.) Butterscotch Morsels
- ½ c. peanut butter

Stir till blended

Remove from heat

ADD and stir till well coated
- 3 c. oven-popped rice cereal

Drop by teaspoonfuls onto waxed paper*

Set in cool place to harden

YIELD: 36 squares

*Or spread in buttered 9″ square pan, cut in 1½″ squares when cool

BUTTERSCOTCH PRALINES

COMBINE in 2-qt. saucepan and bring to *full* boil over high heat, stirring constantly
- 2 c. granulated sugar
- 1 c. firmly packed brown sugar
- ¾ c. water
- ¼ c. light corn syrup
- 1 tsp. vinegar
- ½ tsp. salt

Boil over highest heat 3 min. — *do not stir*

Remove from heat

ADD and stir quickly till butterscotch is melted*
- 1 6-oz. pkg. (1 c.) Butterscotch Morsels
- 1 c. coarsely chopped walnuts

Drop by tablespoonfuls on ungreased foil or heavy brown paper. If mixture becomes too thick, stir in small amount of water

Let stand at room temperature till set

YIELD: approx. 4 dozen

*Mixture is quite thin at this point
(See illustration 11)

BUTTERSCOTCH CRISPIE SQUARES

COMBINE in saucepan
  1 jar marshmallow cream
  2 tbs. water
  2 tbs. corn syrup
Stir constantly over low heat till mixture begins to boil
Remove from heat
ADD and stir till blended and smooth
  2 6-oz. pkgs. (2 c.)
    Butterscotch Morsels
  ½ tsp. vanilla
PLACE in large, greased bowl
  8 c. crisp oven-toasted rice cereal
ADD and stir till blended
  Butterscotch mixture
Press into a well-greased 9" square pan
Chill till firm
Cut into 1½" squares to serve
YIELD: 36 squares

BUTTERSCOTCH PEANUT CRISPS

COMBINE in top of double boiler
  1 6-oz. pkg. (1 c.)
    Butterscotch Morsels
  ½ c. peanut butter
Place over hot (not boiling) water till butterscotch melts. Stir till blended
ADD and stir till well-coated
  1 3-oz. can (2 c.) chow mein noodles
Drop by teaspoonfuls onto waxed paper-lined cookie sheet
Chill till set
YIELD: approx. 3 dozen

Variations: Substitute for noodles *one* of the following:

1. 2 c. broken pretzel sticks
2. 1½ c. raisins
3. 2 c. miniature marshmallows
4. 2 c. broken potato chips
5. 2 c. corn chips
   (See illustrations 26, 27)

BUTTERCHOCS

COMBINE and melt over hot (not boiling) water
  1 6-oz. pkg. (1 c.) Semi-Sweet Chocolate Morsels
  1 6-oz. pkg. (1 c.) Butterscotch Morsels
ADD and mix
  1 3-oz. can chow mein noodles
  1 c. peanuts
Drop by teaspoonfuls on waxed paper-lined cookie sheet. Chill
YIELD: 3½ dozen

HOPSCOTCHERS

MELT over hot (not boiling) water
  1 6-oz. pkg. (1 c.) Butterscotch Morsels
STIR in
  ½ c. peanut butter
MIX together in large bowl
  2 c. chow mein noodles
  2 c. miniature marshmallows
ADD and mix thoroughly
  Butterscotch mixture
Drop by heaping teaspoonfuls onto waxed paper-lined cookie sheet
Chill till set
YIELD: 30

Note: Or spread mixture evenly in greased 9" square pan
Chill till set
Cut in 1½" squares
YIELD: 36 squares

STRAWBERRY CRISPIES

PLACE in greased bowl
  3 c. crisp, puffed cereal
POUR into small bowl
  ¼ c. corn syrup
MIX in gradually
  ½ c. Nestlé's Strawberry Quik
ADD to puffed cereal and mix till well coated
  Quik mixture

Press* into greased 8″ square pan and let stand till set—approx. 1 hr.

Cut in approx. 1¼″ squares

YIELD: 36 squares

*Or drop by tablespoonfuls onto waxed paper and let stand till set
(See illustration 27)

LOLLIPOP MARSHMALLOWS

Lollipop Marshmallows are gaily colored. String them on sticks for candy kabobs or use them to decorate stirrers or straws for drinks.

SOAK in milk for a few minutes
  Marshmallows

STRAWBERRY-FLAVORED: Roll drained marshmallows in Nestlé's Strawberry Quik

CHOCOLATE-FLAVORED: Roll drained marshmallows in mixture of equal parts of Nestlé's Chocolate Quik and sugar

Variations: If desired, coat dry marshmallows with the following liquid mixtures:

1. STRAWBERRY-FLAVORED: Mix 2 tbs. Nestlé's Strawberry Quik with 1 tsp. water and brush over entire surface of marshmallows

2. CHOCOLATE-FLAVORED: Mix 2 tbs. Nestlé's Chocolate Quik with 1 tsp. water and brush over marshmallows

Place coated strawberry or chocolate-flavored marshmallows on waxed paper till surface is dried
(See illustration 26)

CHOCOLATE QUICKIES

COMBINE and place over hot (not boiling) water till chocolate melts
  1 6-oz. pkg. (1 c.) Semi-Sweet
    Chocolate Morsels
  3 tbs. corn syrup
  1 tbs. water
Remove from water
STIR in gently till coated
  2 c. any ready-to-eat cereal

Drop by teaspoonfuls on waxed paper-lined cookie sheet. Chill till firm

YIELD: 2½ to 3 dozen
(See illustration 26)

Variations: Follow basic recipe, omit cereal, and add *one* of the following before dropping on cookie sheet:

1. 1 c. mixed preserved fruits, diced
2. 1½ c. flaked coconut
3. 1 c. dates, chopped
4. 1½ c. raisins
5. 1 c. salted nuts
6. 2 c. small cheese crackers, whole or coarsely crushed
7. 2 c. marshmallows or miniature marshmallows
8. 2 c. pretzel sticks, whole or broken up

YIELD: 2 to 2½ dozen

MOCHA COCONUT PATTIES

COMBINE and cook over moderate heat, stirring constantly, till sugar dissolves and mixture comes to boil

- 1½ c. firmly packed light brown sugar
- 1½ c. coconut
- ¼ tsp. salt
- 2 tbs. Nescafé
- 2 tbs. butter
- ⅓ c. water

Boil 1 min. over moderate heat, stirring constantly

Remove from heat

STIR in till melted

- 1 6-oz. pkg. (1 c.) Semi-Sweet Chocolate Morsels
- ⅛ to ¼ tsp. almond extract

Drop by teaspoonfuls on waxed paper-lined cookie sheet

Chill till firm

YIELD: 4 dozen

(See illustration 6)

SCRABBLE SQUARES

MELT over hot (not boiling) water

- 1 12-oz. pkg. (2 c.) Semi-Sweet Chocolate Morsels
- 2 tbs. shortening

Remove from water

COMBINE in bowl

- 1 6¼-oz. pkg. (approx. 3 c.) miniature marshmallows
- 2 c. coarsely broken pretzels

ADD and fold in carefully till blended

Semi-sweet mixture

Spread evenly in foil-lined 11″ x 7½″ x 1½″ or 9″ square pan

Chill till firm

To serve: Let stand at room temperature a few minutes; remove from pan, then cut into squares

YIELD: 36 to 40 squares

Store in refrigerator

WALNUT CHOCOLETTES

MELT over hot (not boiling) water

- 1 6-oz. pkg. (1 c.) Semi-Sweet Chocolate Morsels

Remove from water

STIR in

- ½ c. sour cream
- ½ c. chopped walnuts
- Dash salt

Chill till firm

COMBINE and mix till crumbly

- 1 c. finely chopped walnuts
- ¼ c. sifted confectioners' sugar
- 1 tbs. soft butter
- 1 tbs. Nestlé's EverReady Cocoa
- 1 tsp. rum extract
- 1 tsp. water
- Dash salt

Form chilled semi-sweet mixture in 1″ balls. Roll balls in crumb mixture. Chill before serving

YIELD: 2 dozen

Store in refrigerator

(See illustrations 10, 11)

page 142 / candies

Christmas Is For Candy

BUTTERSCOTCH APPLES

WASH and stem
6 large or 8 medium apples

INSERT in end of each apple
Wooden skewer or clean twig

COMBINE and set aside
⅓ c. finely crushed ginger snaps
(approx. 8)
¼ tsp. cinnamon

COMBINE in top of 1½-qt. double boiler, and cook over direct moderate heat, stirring constantly till sugar is dissolved
1 c. sugar
⅓ c. water
1 tbs. corn syrup
Bring to full boil
Remove from heat

STIR in till blended
1 6-oz. pkg. (1 c.)
Butterscotch Morsels

DIP apples, one at a time, twirling till well coated in
Butterscotch mixture*

ALLOW excess coating to run off and dip bottoms in
Gingersnap mixture
Place on waxed paper-lined cookie sheet and let stand till coating is firm

YIELD: 6 to 8

*If mixture becomes too thick place over hot water in bottom part of double boiler. Stir till thin enough to re-use

BON BON FUDGE

COMBINE in deep, 3-qt. saucepan and bring to boil, stirring constantly
2½ c. sugar
1¼ c. evaporated milk
Dash salt
Continue boiling for 5 min., stirring up from bottom constantly

STIR in till smooth
1½ 6-oz. pkgs. (1½ c.)
Semi-Sweet Chocolate Morsels
¾ tsp. vanilla
Pour into greased or foil-lined 9″ square pan*

PRESS lightly into the top in 6 rows approx. 1″ apart
12 maraschino cherries, halved, well drained, and dried
6 soft date halves, cut lengthwise
24 salted peanut halves in clusters of 4
6 walnut or pecan halves

TOPPING

MELT over hot (not boiling) water
½ 6-oz. pkg. (½ c.) Semi-Sweet Chocolate Morsels
1½ tbs. shortening
Remove from heat. Spoon semi-sweet mixture over fudge, making sure top is completely coated
Chill till firm
Cut in squares so that each is centered with a piece of fruit or nutmeat

YIELD: approx. 2¾ lbs.
or 36 pieces

*Or pour into greased or foil-lined 10″ round pan and arrange fruits and nuts on top as desired, then cover with semi-sweet Topping

RIBBON CANDIES
STRAWBERRY LAYERS

COMBINE and beat till creamy
- ½ c. soft butter
- 3 tbs. Nestlé's Strawberry Quik
- ½ tsp. lemon or almond extract
- ⅛ tsp. salt

BEAT in gradually
- 2¾ c. sifted confectioners' sugar

KNEAD in
- ½ c. sifted confectioners' sugar

Divide mixture in half

CHOCOLATE LAYERS

Prepare the same as Strawberry Layers but substitute 5 tbs. Nestlé's Chocolate Quik for the Strawberry Quik and substitute ½ tsp. vanilla for the lemon extract

Divide mixture in half

Line a 10" x 5" x 3" pan with foil

Press half the strawberry mixture evenly in bottom of pan. Top with a chocolate layer. Press on remaining halves of each mixture

Cover and chill

Cut in ½" squares and remove from pan

YIELD: approx. 12½ dozen
(See illustrations 10, 11)

NESCAFÉ GLAZED PECANS

COMBINE and boil approx. 3 min., stirring constantly
- 1½ c. pecan halves
- ¼ c. sugar
- 2 tbs. water
- 1 tsp. Nescafé
- ¼ tsp. cinnamon
- Dash salt

Spread on waxed paper to cool
(See illustrations 6, 28)

CHOCOLATE ALMOND BRITTLE

COMBINE in 3-qt. saucepan and cook over moderate heat, stirring constantly till mixture boils
- 2 c. sugar
- 1½ c. butter
- 2 tbs. water
- 1 tbs. Nescafé

Bring to a *full rolling* boil and continue to boil like this for 9 min., stirring from the bottom occasionally

Remove from heat

FOLD in quickly
- 1½ c. blanched, toasted almonds

Spread immediately to a 17" x 14" rectangle on a greased cookie sheet or on greased aluminum foil

Let stand till cool

MELT over hot (not boiling) water
- 1 6-oz. pkg. (1 c.) Semi-Sweet Chocolate Morsels

Spread over cooled toffee

SPRINKLE over semi-sweet
- ½ c. blanched, toasted almonds, finely chopped

Cool thoroughly, then break in irregular pieces

YIELD: 2 lbs.

page 144 | candies

CHOCOLATE-CARAMEL PECAN DROPS

COMBINE and melt over boiling water
¾ lb. vanilla caramels
1 tbs. butter
1 tbs. water

ADD
¾ c. coarsely chopped pecans
Keep warm over hot water

Grease cookie sheet well, then sprinkle with sifted confectioners' sugar

COMBINE and melt over hot (not boiling) water
1 6-oz. pkg. (1 c.) Semi-Sweet Chocolate Morsels
3 tbs. light corn syrup
1 tbs. water
Remove from water

Drop caramel mixture by teaspoonfuls on prepared cookie sheet. Drop semi-sweet mixture by *half* teaspoonfuls on top of caramel mixture
Chill till firm

> **YIELD:** 3½ dozen (approx. 1½ lbs.)

Note: Avoid making in humid weather

BOURBON BALLS

MELT over hot (not boiling) water
1 6-oz. pkg. (1 c.) Semi-Sweet Chocolate Morsels
Remove from water

STIR in
½ c. sugar
3 tbs. light corn syrup

BLEND in
⅓ c. bourbon

COMBINE
2½ c. finely crushed vanilla wafers (approx. 5 dozen)
1 c. walnuts, finely chopped

ADD and mix well
Semi-sweet mixture

Form in 1″ balls. Roll in sugar. Let ripen in covered container at least several days

> **YIELD:** approx. 4½ dozen
> *(See illustrations 10, 11)*

Variation:

ORANGE SUGAR BALLS: Substitute orange juice for bourbon

Note: Bourbon Balls keep for 3 to 4 weeks in a tightly covered container. They improve in flavor on storing

STRAWBERRY FRUIT BALLS

PUT through food chopper, together, using medium blade
2 c. walnuts
1 8-oz. pkg. dates, chopped (1¼ c.)
¾ c. raisins

MIX in thoroughly
¼ c. honey
2 tsp. grated lemon rind
Shape in 1″ balls

ROLL in
¼ c. Nestlé's Strawberry Quik

> **YIELD:** approx. 5 dozen

Variation:

CHOCOLATE FRUIT BALLS:
Substitute for Strawberry Quik:
2 tbs. Nestlé's Chocolate Quik
2 tbs. sugar
Roll Fruit Balls in mixture
(See illustration 11)

SUGAR PLUM TREES

COMBINE and beat till creamy
- ¼ c. soft butter or margarine
- 1 tsp. rum, brandy, or almond extract

BLEND in alternately
- 2 c. sifted confectioners' sugar
- ¼ c. light cream

STIR in
- 3 c. flaked coconut

Drop by heaping teaspoonfuls on waxed paper-lined cookie sheet

Chill till firm enough to handle

Roll each between hands into a ball, then shape into a cone about 1¾" high

Press green-tinted coconut* onto sides to make "trees"

Replace on waxed paper-lined cookie sheet and decorate each with 3 or 4 red cinnamon candies

MELT in small, shallow dish, over hot (not boiling) water, then stir to blend
- ½ 6-oz. pkg. (½ c.) Semi-Sweet Chocolate Morsels
- 1 tbs. shortening

Remove from heat

DIP bottoms of "trees" into
- Melted semi-sweet mixture

Place on waxed paper-lined cookie sheet

Chill till firm

    YIELD: approx. 2 dozen

*To tint coconut:

PLACE in pint jar with cover
- 1 c. flaked coconut

Add gradually few drops green food coloring; cover jar, and shake vigorously after each addition, till coconut is desired color

    (See illustration 26)

CHOCOLATE KING MALLOWS

MELT over hot (not boiling) water—stir till smooth
- 1 9¾-oz. Nestlé's King Size Milk Chocolate Bar (Plain, Almond or Crunch)

Spread in lightly greased 8" or 9" square pan

SPRINKLE with
- 2 c. miniature marshmallows

MELT over hot (not boiling) water—stir till smooth
- 1 12-oz. pkg. (2 c.) Semi-Sweet Chocolate Morsels

SPREAD gently over marshmallows
- Melted semi-sweet

Chill till ready to serve

Cut in squares

    YIELD: 1¾ lbs.

page 146 | candies

COBBLESTONE CANDY

MELT over hot (not boiling) water
   3 6-oz. pkg. (3 c.) Semi-Sweet
      Chocolate Morsels
Stir till smooth

ADD and stir till blended
   2 c. miniature marshmallows
   1 c. coarsely chopped nuts
Spread in foil-lined 8″ square pan
Let stand till firm
Cut in squares

             YIELD: 1⅔ lbs.
(See illustration 26)

TWO-TONE MALLOW BITES
BUTTERSCOTCH LAYER

MELT over hot (not boiling) water;
stir to blend
   2 6-oz. pkgs. (2 c.)
      Butterscotch Morsels
   1 tbs. shortening

ADD
   1 c. chopped walnuts
Spread in greased 9″ square pan

SPRINKLE over Butterscotch Layer
evenly — pressing in gently
   2 c. miniature marshmallows
Cover with

CHOCOLATE LAYER

MELT over hot (not boiling) water
   2 6-oz. pkgs. or 1 12-oz. pkg.
      (2 c.) Semi-Sweet Chocolate
      Morsels
   1 tbs. shortening

SPOON onto and spread evenly over
   Marshmallows
Top with walnut halves, if desired
Cool till firm
Cut in squares

           YIELD: approx. 2 lbs.
(See illustration 10)

PEANUT BUTTER
KING MALLOWS

COMBINE and mix gently; set aside
   2 c. miniature marshmallows*
   ½ c. peanut butter

BREAK in pieces and place over hot
(not boiling) water till bars *just*
begin to melt
   2 9¾-oz. Nestlé's King Size
      Chocolate Bars
      (Milk, Almond, Crunch or
      Fruit 'n Nut)
Remove from heat
Stir till completely melted

SPREAD in a lightly greased 8″
square pan
   One half of the melted chocolate

DROP by teaspoonfuls over choco-
late in pan
   Marshmallow mixture
Spread evenly

SPREAD gently over marshmallow
mixture
   Remaining chocolate
Serve chilled

        YIELD: approx. 1½ lbs.
*Or 16 large marshmallows,
cut in eighths
(See illustration 26)

Wrap your candy in gayly decorated paper and ribbons for glamorous and unusual gifts.

Christmas Tree Box
(3½ yards of ¾" ribbon needed for 6" bow)

Make long loop for center first, then second loop slightly shorter. Turn loops around and make another shorter loop at other side of center. Repeat until tree has enough "branches," then tie "trunk" with narrow strip as shown. Flatten base and tie as shown.

Poinsettia Basket:
(30 inches of 1½" ribbon needed for flower shown)

Fold five 6-inch pieces 1¼" width, four for petals, one for leaves. Cut in shape shown. Moisten center of one pair of petals, attach to second pair; add third and fourth. Fold leaf on angle, moisten and stick to back flower. Cut disc for center, moisten, and attach. Moisten back of poinsettia to attach to box band.

Santa Claus Box • Pompom:
(3 yards 1¼" ribbon needed for bow shown)

For 5-inch pompom, form circle with 11 inches of ribbon, using 1 inch for overlap. Moisten end, attach inside of circle. Make ten layers. Cut, moisten end, and fasten. Flatten circle. Cut wedge-shape pieces at both sides of each fold, leaving ⅛" center. Open circle, put cut-out centers together, tie with narrow strip. To open, slip inner loop out with two fingers, twist down and forward. Repeat till all loops are pulled free.

Santa: (3½ yards of ¾" ribbon needed for 4½-inch Santa)

Make 2-inch Spring for head; 2½-inch Spring for body. Form two straight loops for arms; tie head, arms, and body together. Form slightly longer double loop for legs, moisten and stick together at center. Moisten again and stick to body. Add Shoestring bow tie, hat, bright discs (use nickel for pattern) on hat and body.

candies

Fabulous Foods from Your Freezer

"How did we ever get along without a freezer?" Have you ever asked yourself that question?

Thank heavens, you don't *have* to get along without one these days. Just stock it, and enjoy it. In the modern home a freezer or a freezing compartment in the refrigerator is an appliance as valuable as your stove.

Get into the habit of cooking and baking double amounts, and freezing the additional prepared portion, to be ready for serving when needed. Especially in warm weather, your freezer holds the basics for any pleasant emergency: neighbors who have just dropped in, or your children's friends stopping by. They will welcome the refreshment you can so easily serve at a moment's notice. Each time you wheel out your cart with its assortment of desserts and beverages, you'll bless your freezer — and your own foresight.

Not the least of its many advantages are the ice creams and sherbets your freezer can hold until you want them. Buy — or make — a generous supply to have on hand when your teenager's gang descends. Just line up batches of assorted sundae sauces, set out the makings for sodas, and let them dig in. They'll stack up the records, and you'll have a home where they'll love to meet.

For the littlest, you'll find a gay collection of fun-filled treats — frozen pops, chilled frosteds, and lots more.

Your own dinner parties and luncheons will be enhanced by the addition of beautiful desserts you have made in advance. Try the Frozen Cream Chiffon Roll. Make it in the cool of the morning, store it, and serve it without bother or fuss — then wait for the compliments.

You'll treasure these fabulous foods from your freezer. They're convenient, they're glamorous — and they're *easy*.

Frozen Dessert Delights

CHOCOLATE ICE CREAM
COMBINE and bring to boil
   1 14-oz. can (1¼ c.)
      sweetened condensed milk
   2 tbs. corn syrup
   ⅛ tsp. salt
Remove from heat
ADD and stir till smooth
   1 6-oz. pkg. (1 c.) Nestlé's
      Semi-Sweet Chocolate
      Morsels
BEAT in, one at a time
   2 egg yolks
BLEND in
   1¼ c. water
   2 tsp. vanilla
Freeze in refrigerator trays till *just* frozen
BEAT till stiff but not dry
   2 egg whites
BEAT in till stiff and glossy
   2 tbs. sugar
STIR in *chilled* bowl till smooth but not melted
   Semi-sweet mixture
FOLD in
   Egg white mixture
Return to refrigerator trays
Freeze till firm
      YIELD: 6 to 8 servings

CHOCOLATE IGLOOS
Have ready 8 dessert shells
MELT over hot (not boiling) water
   1 6-oz. pkg. (1 c.) Semi-Sweet
      Chocolate Morsels
DIP top and sides of dessert shells in
   Melted semi-sweet
ROLL coated dessert shells in
   ½ c. finely chopped nuts or
      packaged, grated coconut
Chill till chocolate sets
FILL each shell with
   Scoop of ice cream
      YIELD: 8 servings

NESCAFÉ TORTONI
Set control of refrigerator at coldest point
COMBINE and beat till foamy
   1 egg white
   1½ tsp. Nescafé
   ⅛ tsp. salt
BEAT in gradually and continue beating till stiff peaks form
   2 tbs. sugar
COMBINE and beat till stiff
   1 c. heavy cream
   ¼ c. sugar
   1 tsp. vanilla
   ⅛ tsp. almond extract
FOLD in
   Egg-white mixture
   ¼ c. blanched toasted almonds,
      finely chopped
Spoon into eight 2-oz. paper cups
Freeze till firm
      YIELD: 8 servings
   (See illustration 19)

page 150 / freezer

FROZEN CREAM CHIFFON ROLL
ROLL

Preheat oven to 350°F.

PREPARE according to label directions

    1 pkg. chiffon cake mix

Pour into a 15″ x 10″ x 1″ pan, lined with greased, waxed paper

BAKE at: 350°F.

TIME: 30 to 40 min.

Loosen around edges and turn out on towel sprinkled with confectioners' sugar. Remove paper; trim off edges. Roll cake immediately in towel

Cool

Prepare

FILLING

COMBINE and bring *just* to boil over moderate heat stirring constantly

    2 tbs. honey

    1½ tsp. water

Remove from heat

STIR in till smooth

    ½ 6-oz. pkg. (½ c.) Semi-Sweet Chocolate Morsels

    ½ tsp. vanilla

Cool approx. 10 min.

FOLD in

    ¾ c. heavy cream, whipped

Chill till thick enough to spread

Unroll cake, spread with Filling; roll up again

Chill for several hours or wrap in foil and freeze

To serve: Sprinkle with confectioners' sugar. Cut in slices

        YIELD: approx. 14 servings
(See illustration 20)

CHOCO-PINEAPPLE FROSTIES

DRAIN, and dry chunks between paper towels

    1 No. 2 can pineapple chunks*

STRING on wooden sticks or skewers

    4 or 5 pineapple chunks

Freeze

COMBINE and melt over hot (not boiling) water

    1 6-oz. pkg. (1 c.) Semi-Sweet Chocolate Morsels

    1 tbs. vegetable shortening

Remove from heat

COAT each stick of frozen pineapple chunks with

    Melted semi-sweet

Wrap in aluminum foil and store in freezer

        YIELD: approx. 12

*Use drained and well-dried canned pineapple spears, fresh apple, pear or thick banana slices

MOCHA DELIGHT FREEZE

COMBINE in pan and bring to *full* boil over low heat, stirring constantly
- 1 c. Nestlé's EverReady Cocoa
- ¼ c. corn syrup
- ¼ c. water
- 1 tsp. Nescafé

ADD and stir till blended
- 2 tbs. butter

Remove from heat and cool

COMBINE in large bowl and chill thoroughly
- 1½ c. heavy cream
- Cocoa mixture
- ⅔ c. sweetened condensed milk
- ½ tsp. vanilla

Whip till fluffy and soft peaks form

Pile into refrigerator tray or 10" x 5" x 3" pan

Freeze till firm

YIELD: 8 to 10 servings

FRENCH MOCHA ICE CREAM

BEAT till thick and lemon colored
- 2 egg yolks
- ¼ tsp. salt

Bring to *full* boil over medium heat, stirring constantly
- ⅓ c. corn syrup

BEAT syrup gradually into
- Egg-yolk mixture

Continue beating till mixture is very stiff

COMBINE in top of double boiler
- 1 6-oz. pkg. (1 c.) Semi-Sweet Chocolate Morsels
- 2 tbs. hot water
- ½ tsp. Nescafé

Place over boiling water. Stir constantly till smooth and blended

ADD to egg-yolk mixture
- Semi-sweet mixture

FOLD in
- 2 c. heavy cream, whipped

Pour into two refrigerator trays and freeze till firm

YIELD: 8 to 10 servings

FROZEN CHOCOLATE PUFFS

Have ready 8 medium cream puff shells

COMBINE in pan and place over moderate heat, stirring constantly till melted
- ½ lb. (32) marshmallows
- ⅓ c. water
- ¼ tsp. salt

Remove from heat

ADD and stir till melted
- 1 6-oz. pkg. (1 c.) Semi-Sweet Chocolate Morsels

Cool approx. 15 min.

FOLD in
- 1 c. heavy cream, whipped
- ⅛ tsp. almond extract

Cut tops from cream puffs. Fill generously with chocolate mixture and replace tops

Wrap in foil and freeze till ready to serve

YIELD: 8 puffs

page 152 / freezer

CHOCOLATE GRAHAM LOAF

MELT over hot (not boiling) water
    1 6-oz. pkg. (1 c.) Semi-Sweet
       Chocolate Morsels
Remove from water

ADD and stir till smooth
    ½ c. corn syrup
    2 tbs. water

RESERVE for glaze
    ¼ c. semi-sweet mixture

FOLD into remaining semi-sweet
    1 c. heavy cream, whipped
    1 tsp. vanilla

PLACE in bottom of waxed paper-
lined 10″ x 5″ x 3″ pan
    5 graham crackers, broken
       in large pieces

POUR over
    ⅓ semi-sweet mixture
Repeat in layers, finishing with
graham crackers

DRIZZLE over top
    Reserved semi-sweet mixture
Freeze till firm
Wrap and store in freezer

To serve: Lift from pan. Remove
waxed paper. Cut in half, lengthwise, then crosswise in 2″ slices

        YIELD: 20 servings

FROZEN STRAWBERRY MOUSSE

COMBINE in large mixing bowl
    1½ c. heavy cream
    ⅔ c. sweetened condensed milk
    ½ c. Strawberry Sauce
     (see page 132)

Chill thoroughly

Beat till thick and soft peaks form

Pile into refrigerator tray or a
10″ x 5″ x 3″ pan

Freeze till firm

        YIELD: 8 to 10 servings

FROZEN CHOCOLATE MOUSSE

COMBINE and bring *just* to boil over
moderate heat, stirring constantly
    ¼ c. dark corn syrup
    1 tbs. water
Remove from heat

ADD and stir till smooth
    1 6-oz. pkg. (1 c.) Semi-Sweet
       Chocolate Morsels
    1 tbs. vanilla
Cool

COMBINE in large mixing bowl
    1½ c. heavy cream
    Semi-sweet mixture
    ⅔ c. sweetened condensed milk

Chill thoroughly

Beat till thick and soft peaks form

FOLD in
    ½ c. toasted slivered almonds

Pour into refrigerator tray or
10″ x 5″ x 3″ pan

Freeze till firm

        YIELD: 8 to 10 servings

22 Something special for teenage "record hops": *(from top to bottom)* Calypso Shake (p. 182) with a Jumbo Bar (p. 53) and a Scandinavian Snapper (p. 65); Strawberry Flip (p. 182), a Chocolate Crackler (p. 60) and a Jumbo Bar; Raspberry Shrub (p. 179), a Scandinavian Snapper and a Chocolate Crackler.

23 Frostings with a flair: bowls of Fluffy Strawberry Frosting (p. 26), Chocolate Cream Frosting (p. 22) and Cocoa Cream Frosting (p. 23). They, as well as Butterscotch Butter Frosting (p. 24), frost the Devil's Delight Cupcakes (p. 9). The loaf cake is iced with Feathered Frosting (p. 27). Chocolate Fondant Glaze (p. 22) tops the petits fours.

24 The perfect beginning for a perfect day—a continental breakfast of Rich Hot Chocolate (p. 175) with flaky brioche.

25 For a festive Fourth of July—or for any summer evening—a heaping bowl of vanilla ice cream with: *(top shelf, from left to right)* Chocolate Marshmallow Sauce (p. 131), Skillet Sundae Sauce (p. 166), Chocolate Peanut Sauce (p. 129), Strawberry Sauce (p. 132). On the bottom shelf: Butterscotch Sundae Sauce (p. 167), Strawberry Quik Soda (p. 164), Minty Way (p. 182).

26 On the Christmas tree *(upper left)* hang Namesake Cookies (p. 87); spread around it: Pink Party Punch (p. 182), Lollipop Marshmallows (p. 140), Holiday Fruit Cake (p. 16). In the jar: *(from top to bottom)* Cobblestone Candies (p. 146), Butterscotch Peanut Crisps (p. 139) and Peanut Butter King Mallows (p. 146). In the dish: *(from left to right)* Chocolate Lebkuchen (p. 65), Festive Clusters (p. 58), Chocolate Quickies (p. 140), Sugar Plum Trees (p. 145).

27 Sure to be a hit at any children's party: graham-cracker Stackmores (p. 109), Deluxe Chocolate Pops (p. 162), Butterscotch Peanut Crisps (p. 139), Strawberry Crispies (p. 140) and *(on skewers in the orange)* Frozen Banana Kabobs (p. 163). Beverages are: *(top to bottom)* Strawberry Sparkler (p. 181), Fruity Quik Milk "Shake" (p. 165) and Brown Cow (p. 164).

28 A drink for every occasion: *(from the flaming cup clockwise)* Brûlot Nescafé (p. 171), Piquant Mulled Tea (p. 178), 2 cups of Café Cointreau (p. 170), Gold Coast Gaiety (p. 170), Café Cacao (p. 173), Mocha Dilly (p. 172), West Indian Julep (p. 171) and Australian Coffee Foam (p. 172). In the center: Nescafé Glazed Pecans (p. 143).

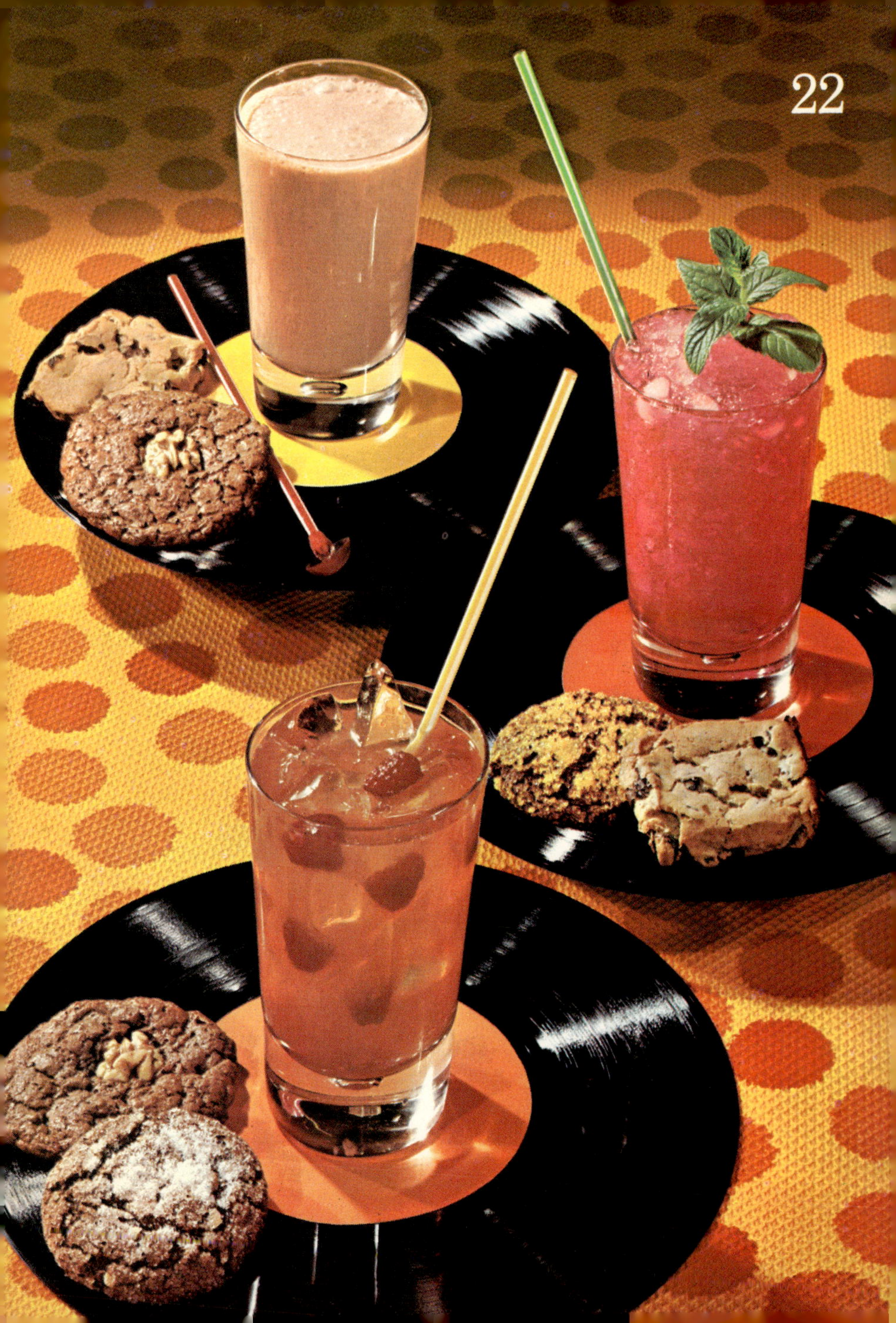
22

23

24

25

26

27

28

ORANGE-CHOCOLATE MOUSSE

COMBINE in saucepan and bring to *full* boil over low heat, stirring constantly
- ¾ c. Nestlé's Chocolate Quik
- ¼ c. light corn syrup
- ¼ c. water

STIR in till blended
- 2 tbs. butter

Remove from heat

Cool

COMBINE and chill
- 1½ c. heavy cream
- Quik mixture
- ⅔ c. sweetened condensed milk
- ½ tsp. vanilla

Beat till thick, and soft peaks form

FOLD in
- 1 tbs. grated orange rind

Turn into refrigerator tray or 10" x 5" x 3" pan

Freeze till firm

YIELD: 8 to 10 servings

COMBINE and melt over hot (not boiling) water
- 1 6-oz. pkg. (1 c.) Semi-Sweet Chocolate Morsels
- 2 tbs. shortening

Turn frozen mixture into chilled bowl and stir till smooth but not melted

STIR in slowly, by drizzling*
- Melted semi-sweet

Return to refrigerator tray and continue to freeze till firm

YIELD: 8 servings

*This "chips" the semi-sweet

Variation:

PINK PEPPERMINT "CHIP"

Omit orange juice

ADD
- ⅛ tsp. peppermint extract
- ⅛ tsp. red food coloring

ORANGE "CHIP" DESSERT

COMBINE and let stand 5 min.
- ¼ c. cold water
- 1 envelope unflavored gelatin

Dissolve over hot water

COMBINE and mix well
- 2 c. milk
- 1½ c. light corn syrup
- 1 6-oz. can frozen orange juice concentrate, thawed
- Dissolved gelatin

Pour in one large or two small refrigerator trays

Freeze till *just* frozen

Treats for Tots

QUIK COVERED POPS

COMBINE and bring to full boil, stirring constantly
    ½ c. Nestlé's Chocolate Quik
    2 tbs. water
Remove from heat

STIR in till melted
    3 tbs. shortening
Reserve 2 tbs.

DIVIDE in four 4-oz. paper cups
    Remaining Quik mixture

Let cool 5 min.

Rotate cups back and forth to coat entire inside surfaces. Chill till firm — approx. 10 min.

PACK in each cup
    ½ c. vanilla ice cream, slightly softened

SPREAD over tops of cups to cover ice cream
    Reserved Quik mixture

Insert a lollipop stick in each cup. Freeze till firm. Then wrap properly for freezing

To serve: Tear off paper cups — serve immediately

YIELD: 4 pops

DELUXE CHOCOLATE POPS

MIX in small saucepan
    ⅓ c. Nestlé's Chocolate Quik
    1½ tsp. unflavored gelatin

STIR in gradually
    ¼ c. milk

Place over low heat. Stir till gelatin dissolves

ADD and chill till slightly thickened
    1¾ c. milk
Stir slightly
Insert sticks in 6 molds

FILL with
    Quik mixture
Freeze

YIELD: 6 pops

(See illustration 27)

CHOCOLATE POPS

COMBINE in pitcher; mix thoroughly
    2 c. milk
    ⅓ c. Nestlé's Chocolate Quik
Insert sticks in 6 molds

FILL with
    Quik mixture
Freeze

YIELD: 6 pops

Variation:

STRAWBERRY POPS: Substitute ¼ c. Nestlés Strawberry Quik for Chocolate Quik

BUTTERSCOTCH-PEANUT BANANA POPS

CUT in halves, crosswise
  6 peeled, ripe bananas

Insert a wooden stick into the cut end of each banana

Freeze

MELT over hot (not boiling) water
  1 6-oz. pkg. (1 c.) Nestlé's Butterscotch Morsels
  ½ c. peanut butter

Stir till blended and smooth

Remove from heat

COAT each frozen banana half with Butterscotch-peanut butter mixture

Wrap in foil and store in freezer

YIELD: 12 pops

FROZEN BANANA KABOBS

CUT in fourths or fifths
  6 peeled ripe bananas

String 2 or 3 banana pieces on wooden skewers or sticks

Freeze

MELT over hot (not boiling) water
  1 6-oz. pkg. (1 c.) Semi-Sweet Chocolate Morsels
  1 tbs. shortening

SPREAD bananas with
  Melted semi-sweet

Wrap each kabob in foil and return to freezer

YIELD: 8 to 15

(See illustration 27)

DELUXE STRAWBERRY POPS

MIX in small saucepan
  ¼ c. Nestlé's Strawberry Quik
  1½ tsp. unflavored gelatin

STIR in gradually
  ½ c. milk

Place over low heat. Stir till gelatin dissolves

ADD and chill till slightly thickened
  1½ c. milk

Stir slightly

Insert sticks in 6 molds

FILL with
  Quik mixture

Freeze

YIELD: 6 pops

STRAWBERRY-PINEAPPLE PARFAIT

PLACE in bottom of tall ice cream dish
  1 scoop ice cream

ADD
  1 tbs. drained, crushed pineapple

SPRINKLE with
  1 heaping tsp. Nestlé's Strawberry Quik

Repeat layers three times

TOP with
  1 scoop ice cream

YIELD: 1 serving

page 164 | freezer

À LA MODE SANDWICHES

HAVE ready 1 qt. softened ice cream

CUT in half crosswise
8 doughnuts

SANDWICH each 2 halves together with
½ c. softened ice cream

Place on foil and freeze, then wrap and store in freezer till ready to use

Remove from freezer 10 min. before serving

Prepare

Hot Fudge Sauce *(see page 131)*

Serve hot on doughnut-ice cream sandwiches

YIELD: 8 servings

The New Old-Fashioned Ice-Cream Parlor

BROWN COW

EMPTY into a tall glass
1 6-oz. bottle cola-flavored beverage

ADD
2 heaping tsp. Nestlé's Chocolate Quik

Stir till dissolved

ADD
2 scoops vanilla ice cream

Stir quickly till foamy

Serve at once

YIELD: 1 serving
(See illustration 27)

CHOCOLATE QUIK SODA

PLACE in tall glass
3 heaping tsp. Nestlé's Chocolate Quik

STIR in
Small amount of milk

ADD
Scoop of ice cream

FILL with
Chilled soda

YIELD: 1 serving

STRAWBERRY QUIK SODA

COMBINE in a tall glass
3 heaping tsp. Nestlé's Strawberry Quik
Small amount of milk

ADD
1 scoop softened strawberry or vanilla ice cream

FILL slowly with
Chilled sparkling water

YIELD: 1 serving
(See illustration 25)

NESCAFÉ SODA

COMBINE in tall glass
1 tbs. sugar
1 tsp. Nescafé

ADD gradually, stirring till dissolved
½ c. milk, or milk to fill half glass

ADD
1 scoop (approx. ½ c.) softened vanilla ice cream

FILL slowly with
Chilled sparkling water

YIELD: 1 serving

STRAWBERRY DOUBLE-FROSTED

COMBINE and beat till smooth
 ½ pt. softened vanilla ice cream
 ¼ c. Nestlé's Strawberry Quik

ADD and beat well
 3 c. cold milk

Pour into 4 tall glasses

To serve: Top each glass with one small scoop vanilla ice cream

YIELD: 4 servings

COFFEE MILK SHAKE

COMBINE and mix well
 ½ c. milk
 1½ tsp. Nescafé

ADD and mix just enough to blend
 2 to 3 large scoops vanilla ice cream*

YIELD: 1 serving

*Depending on thickness desired

FRUITY QUIK MILK "SHAKE"

COMBINE in tall glass
 3 heaping tsp. Nestlé's Chocolate Quik
 2 to 3 canned peach slices, mashed
 2 tbs. peach syrup

Mix well

ADD
 1 scoop softened vanilla ice cream (approx. ½ c.)

FILL with
 Cold milk

Variation:

Substitute 2 to 3 tbs. crushed pineapple, undrained, for peaches and syrup

(See illustration 27)

CHOCO-BERRY FIZZ

COMBINE and dissolve
 2 c. milk
 ½ c. Nestlé's Strawberry Quik
 ⅓ c. Nestlé's Chocolate Quik

Pour mixture in four (12-oz.) glasses

ADD to each
 1 scoop of ice cream

FILL up with
 Chilled sparkling or soda water

YIELD: 4 servings

A perfect way for teen-agers to get together is a make-it-yourself sundae party. These sauces, of course, are not strictly "from your freezer," but in most cases, they can be prepared in advance and stored in your refrigerator—for use with ice cream —or on cake or pudding, if you prefer.

page 166 | *freezer*

HURRY-UP QUIK SAUCE

PLACE in cup
3 heaping tsp. Nestlé's Chocolate
or Strawberry Quik
STIR in gradually, till smooth, and
of desired consistency
Hot tap water
Serve at once over ice cream

YIELD: 1 serving

COCOA-MALLOW SUNDAE SAUCE

COMBINE in saucepan
½ c. Nestlé's EverReady Cocoa
½ c. sugar
½ c. evaporated milk
Bring *just* to boil over moderate
heat, stirring constantly
Remove from heat
ADD just before serving
½ c. miniature marshmallows
Serve warm or cool over ice cream
or warm cake

YIELD: approx. 1¼ c.

SKILLET SUNDAE SAUCE

MELT in heavy skillet
¼ c. butter
ADD and stir constantly over moderate heat till nicely browned
1 c. coarsely chopped walnuts
Remove from heat
ADD and stir till melted and smooth
1 6-oz. pkg. (1 c.) Semi-Sweet
Chocolate Morsels
Serve warm over ice cream or warm
cake squares

YIELD: 1¼ c.

Note: Reheat cooled sauce over hot
water

(See illustration 25)

SPEEDY COFFEE SAUCE

COMBINE and bring to boil, stirring
constantly
½ c. light corn syrup
1 tbs. water
1½ tsp. Nescafé
Dash salt
Continue boiling for 1 min.
Serve hot or cold over ice cream

YIELD: ½ c.

THIN CHOCOLATE SAUCE

COMBINE and stir over moderate
heat till blended and smooth
1 6-oz. pkg. (1 c.) Semi-Sweet
Chocolate Morsels
¼ c. water
STIR in gradually
½ c. evaporated milk
¼ c. water
Store covered, in refrigerator

YIELD: 1½ c.

Serve on ice cream or cake or use
to make milk shakes, sodas or floats

BUTTERSCOTCH SUNDAE SAUCE

MIX in saucepan
  2 tsp. cornstarch
  ¼ tsp. salt
COMBINE and stir in gradually
  ¾ c. orange juice
  ½ c. corn syrup
  ⅛ tsp. peppermint extract

Cook over moderate heat till slightly thickened, stirring constantly

ADD and stir till melted
  1 6-oz. pkg. (1 c.)
    Butterscotch Morsels

Remove from heat

ADD and stir till partially dissolved
  1 c. miniature marshmallows

Serve warm over ice cream or cake. If sauce becomes too thick, reheat over hot water

YIELD: 2 c.

(See illustration 25)

COFFEE SUNDAE SAUCE

MIX till Nescafé dissolves
  1 tbs. Nescafé
  1 tsp. warm water
STIR in
  1 c. sweetened condensed milk
  Dash salt

Spoon over ice cream

YIELD: 1 c.

EVERREADY SUNDAE SAUCE

COMBINE in saucepan and bring *just* to boil, stirring constantly
  ½ c. evaporated milk
  ½ c. corn syrup
ADD to, gradually, stirring till well blended after each addition
  ½ c. Nestlé's EverReady Cocoa

YIELD: 1 c.

FUDGE SUNDAE SAUCE

COMBINE and bring *just* to boil, over low heat, stirring constantly
  ½ c. corn syrup*
  ½ c. evaporated milk
  2 tbs. water

Remove from heat

ADD at once, stirring till blended and smooth
  1 6-oz. pkg. (1 c.) Semi-Sweet
    Chocolate Morsels
  1 tsp. vanilla

Serve warm over ice cream or warm cake

YIELD: 1⅔ c.

Note: Sauce may be reheated over hot water

*For maple-flavored sauce, substitute maple-blended syrup for corn syrup

Beverages —Plain and Fancy

Coffee and tea, cocoa and milk—all these are staples of American homes. But what a wealth of enjoyment can be created by combining them with the magic ingredient of imagination!

Coffee, for instance, is perfect for providing that extra pleasure to after-dinner hours spent with friends and family. Conversation seems to flow more easily over coffee, doesn't it? When the coffee itself is a delicious concoction served in a brandy snifter, it can substitute for a more elaborate dessert.

Most Americans traveling in Europe for the first time are impressed by the charm of the many coffee-houses, where one can sit comfortably, and watch the world go by. Here at home, coffee and conversation can create the same unhurried atmosphere.

Another old-world custom which might be practiced more by Americans is the gracious one of afternoon tea. Whether you pour your tea into pottery mugs or the finest of china, the rewards are many. Certainly, for the harried mother of active youngsters, a quiet cup of tea, alone or shared with a neighbor, provides a welcome break in her all-too-rushed and *un*quiet day.

Then there are the gala occasions. A sweet sixteen party calls for a frothy pink cooler set in a beautiful bowl. Sparkling punch floated with ice cream is exactly the special touch for small-fry. These, along with candy and cookies, spell "party" to every youngster we know. There will be many other instances when your own family's interests will suggest uses for zesty punches and brews.

Even at breakfast—the simplest of meals—a pot of steaming cocoa on the table will set the tone. Remember that for getting everyone off to a warm, well-fed start, nothing takes the place of a good breakfast. So have a good breakfast—and have a good day!

Coffee 'Round the World

The story of coffee is a romantic pageant that began before 1000 A.D. when it was first used in Arabia. Carried by traders and soldiers of fortune, it traveled the trade routes to Turkey.

Returning Crusaders brought coffee to Venice. And by the time bloody Ottoman invaders had beseiged Vienna and other European capitals in the 16th Century, coffee already was a widely-used beverage.

Before coffee achieved its status as a household standby, it was served solely in public coffee houses. Will's Coffee House of London, for one, was a popular meeting place for such writers as Sheridan, Swift, Johnson, Goldsmith, Addison, Steele, and others. These literary giants often wrote about coffee as a stimulating part of their stimulating lives.

Early Americans turned to coffee after tea had lost much of its popularity following the famed Boston Tea Party (which, incidentally, was plotted in a coffee house!).

We have been a nation of coffee drinkers ever since. From our earliest days, a pot of coffee warming on the back of the kitchen stove has been an American tradition.

As our country has grown, so has the art of coffee drinking. In recent years, the "coffee break," an American innovation that has its roots in the *kaffee klatches* of early Vienna, has become part of our everyday social and business life.

Just before World War II a new coffee development started it on the road to even greater popularity. The Nestlé Company in Switzerland originated Nescafé®, an instant coffee that gives a true-flavor cup of coffee in seconds.

Today instant coffee is a staple in homes everywhere, a drink that is as socially acceptable as any served. About one cup of coffee in every three now used is instant coffee and Nescafé has led the way in this coffee drinking revolution.

COFFEE COOLERS
COMBINE in each julep glass
    ¼ c. light rum
    2 tbs. Simple Syrup *(see page 171)*
    ½ tsp. Nescafé
Fill with cracked ice

                 YIELD: 2 servings

HAWAIIAN COOLERS

COMBINE
  ¼ c. Nescafé
  ½ c. sugar

ADD gradually, stirring
  2 c. pineapple juice
  1 c. water
  ½ c. curacao
Pour in six 7-oz. stem glasses
Fill with cracked ice
YIELD: 6 servings

CAFÉ COINTREAU FOR TWO

COMBINE
  1 tbs. Nescafé
  1½ c. boiling water
  ¼ c. (2 oz.) cointreau
Pour into two 9-oz. mugs

ADD to each mug
  1 thin strip lemon peel, twisted
YIELD: 2 servings
(See illustration 28)

COFFEE BANANA COOLER

COMBINE in tall glass and stir
till dissolved
  2 tsp. Nescafé
  2 tsp. sugar
  2 tbs. milk

ADD and stir well
  ½ banana, mashed

FILL with
  Cold milk
YIELD: 1 serving

GOLD COAST GAIETY

COMBINE in each of two 9-oz. mugs
  1 tbs. Nescafé
  3 tbs. Nestlé's EverReady Cocoa
  1 c. boiling water
Top with whipped cream
YIELD: 2 servings
(See illustration 28)

CAFÉ AU LAIT

COMBINE
  ¼ c. Nescafé
  2 c. boiling water
  2 c. scalded milk (heated to *just*
    below boiling point)

TOP with
  Whipped cream
YIELD: 4 servings

HONEYPOT COFFEE

COMBINE and bring to a full boil
  ¾ c. water
  1 tbs. sesame seeds
  2 tbs. honey
Cover and simmer 5 minutes

Remove from heat

ADD
  2 tbs. Nescafé

Strain into two demi-tasse cups
YIELD: 2 servings

CREAMY NESCAFÉ

BLEND in 1½-qt. container
  3 to 4 tbs. Nescafé
  ¼ c. hot water

ADD and stir to blend
  1 14-oz. can (1¼ c.)
    sweetened condensed milk
  Cold water enough to fill
    container
  ¼ tsp. flavoring extract*
Cover and chill
YIELD: 4 large or 8
  small servings
*Or omit extract and

STIR into each glass
  3 tbs. finely mashed banana

BRÛLOT NESCAFÉ

COMBINE in Brûlot bowl
    1 orange peel, cut in thin strips
    1 lemon peel, cut in thin strips
    4 1" sticks cinnamon
    1 tbs. whole cloves
    24 sugar cubes

COMBINE in coffee server
    6 tbs. Nescafé
    4 c. boiling water

POUR over sugar mixture —
do not stir
    ¾ c. brandy

Ignite and let burn. Ladle carefully flaming brandy over mixture several minutes till flame burns out

ADD
    Nescafé mixture
        to
    Brandy mixture

Strain if desired and ladle into demi-tasse cups

    YIELD: approx. 12 3-oz. servings
        (See illustration 28)

WEST INDIAN JULEPS

COMBINE in each of four julep glasses
    2 tbs. lemon juice
    2 tbs. Simple Syrup*
    ¼ c. light rum
    1 tsp. Nescafé

FILL with
    Cracked ice

    YIELD: 4 servings

*SIMPLE SYRUP

Bring to boil, then chill
    ⅓ c. sugar
    ⅓ c. water
        (See illustration 28)

COFFEE MALLOW SMOOTHIE

COMBINE and stir till blended
    ¼ c. boiling water
    2 to 3 tbs. Nescafé
    ¼ tsp. almond extract
    ⅛ tsp. salt

OPEN
    1 jar marshmallow cream

BLEND in
    Nescafé mixture

Pour into 1½-qt. covered refrigerator container

ADD and stir to blend
    3 c. milk
    ½ c. heavy cream

Chill

Shake well before serving

    YIELD: 4 servings

page 172 | *beverages*

MOCHA DILLY

DISSOLVE
1 tsp. Nescafé
in
1 tbs. boiling water

COMBINE in blender
1 c. crushed ice
1 large scoop vanilla ice cream
⅓ c. crème de cacao
Nescafé mixture
1 tsp. white crème de menthe

Cover and blend at high speed till ice is finely crushed — about 60 seconds

Serve in 5-oz. glasses

YIELD: 4 servings
(See illustration 28)

AUSTRALIAN COFFEE FOAM

COMBINE and beat till thick
2 egg yolks
⅓ c. Nescafé
1 tbs. vanilla
Dash salt

BEAT in gradually till *very* thick
¼ c. sugar

STIR in gradually
¾ c. brandy
2 c. milk

Chill thoroughly

BEAT till stiff but not dry
2 egg whites

BEAT in gradually till stiff and satiny
½ c. sugar

FOLD into Nescafé mixture
Egg white mixture
1 c. heavy cream, whipped

Serve in 5-oz. glasses with small spoons or plastic straws

YIELD: approx. 13 servings
(See illustration 28)

ARABIAN COFFEE

For each serving

COMBINE in coffee cup
2 tsp. Nescafé
4 tsp. brown sugar
Dash cinnamon
Dash nutmeg
Small amount of water

STIR in slowly to fill cup
Boiling water
or
Hot milk*

*Heat till *just* below boiling point

YIELD: 1 serving

SYRIAN COFFEE

COMBINE and bring to a full boil
⅔ c. water
2 cardamon seeds, crushed

Remove from heat

ADD and stir
2 tsp. Nescafé

Strain into demi-tasse cups

YIELD: 2 servings
(approx. ⅓ c. each)

CAFÉ CACAO

COMBINE
  4 tsp. Nescafé
  1½ c. boiling water
  ¼ c. (2 oz.) crème de cacao
Pour into two 9-oz. coffee mugs

TOP with
  Whipped cream

YIELD: 2 servings

(See illustration 28)

CAFÉ CACAO FRAPPÉ

COMBINE and stir briskly
  4 tsp. Nescafé
  1 c. water
  ¼ c. crème de cacao

Freeze till *just* frozen

Pour in frappé glasses

TOP with
  Sweetened whipped cream

Serve with straws

YIELD: 3 servings

CREAMY CAFÉ FLOAT

COMBINE in tall glass and stir till dissolved
  1 tsp. Nescafé
  2 tbs. marshmallow cream
  Small amount of hot water

ADD
  1 scoop softened vanilla ice cream (approx. ½ c.)

FILL with
  Cold milk

If desired, add 1 or 2 drops almond extract

CAFÉ CARIBE

COMBINE in saucepan
  2 tbs. Nescafé
  2 tbs. boiling water
  2 tbs. dark brown sugar

ADD and bring *just* to a boil
  1½ c. milk

Serve in 9-oz. coffee mugs

YIELD: 2 servings

page 174 / beverages

NESCAFÉ

GROUP SERVINGS

SERVINGS	DIRECTIONS	AMOUNTS OF BOILING WATER	NESCAFÉ
HOT NESCAFÉ			
Single	PLACE Nescafé in cup. ADD boiling water. Stir and serve.	5 ozs.	1 rounded tsp.
28	EMPTY Nescafé into large vessel. ADD boiling water. Stir. Steep 5 minutes and serve.	5¼ qts. or 1¼ gals.	2-oz. jar
56	EMPTY Nescafé into large vessel. ADD boiling water. Stir. Steep 5 minutes and serve.	10½ qts. or 2½ gals.	Two 2-oz. jars
84	EMPTY Nescafé into large vessel. ADD boiling water. Stir. Steep 5 minutes and serve.	15¾ qts. or 4 gals.	6-oz. jar
140	EMPTY Nescafé into large vessel. ADD boiling water. Stir. Steep 5 minutes and serve.	26¼ qts. or 6½ gals.	10-oz. jar
ICED NESCAFÉ		COLD WATER	NESCAFÉ
Single	PLACE Nescafé in tall glass. Add cold tap water and stir. ADD ice and water to fill glass.	½ c. (plus ice and water to fill glass)	2 rounded tsp.
18	POUR into large vessel .... ADD Nescafé; stir till dissolved. Serve over ice in tall glasses. Pass sugar and cream, if desired.	4½ qts.	2-oz. jar
36	POUR into large vessel .... ADD Nescafé and stir till dissolved. STIR in additional water .... Serve over ice in tall glasses (mixture will be foamy on top, at first). Pass sugar and cream, if desired.	1 qt. 8 qts.	Two 2-oz. jars
54	POUR into large vessel .... ADD Nescafé and stir till dissolved. STIR in additional water .... Serve over ice in tall glasses (mixture will be foamy on top, at first). Pass sugar and cream, if desired.	1 qt. 12½ qts.	6-oz. jar
90	POUR into large vessel .... ADD Nescafé and stir till dissolved. STIR in additional water .... Serve over ice in tall glasses (mixture will be foamy on top, at first). Pass sugar and cream, if desired.	1 qt. 20½ qts.	10-oz. jar

DECAF

GROUP SERVINGS

SERVINGS	DIRECTIONS	AMOUNTS OF BOILING WATER	DECAF
HOT DECAF			
Single	PLACE Decaf in cup. ADD boiling water; stir and serve.	5 ozs.	1 rounded tsp.
32	EMPTY Decaf into large vessel. ADD boiling water and stir. Steep 5 minutes and serve.	5¼ qts.	2-oz. jar
70	EMPTY Decaf into large vessel. ADD boiling water and stir. Steep 5 minutes and serve.	3⅓ gals.	5-oz. jar
ICED DECAF		**COLD WATER**	**DECAF**
Single	PLACE Decaf in tall glass. ADD ice and water to fill glass.	½ c. (plus ice and water to fill glass)	2 rounded tsp.
18	POUR cold tap water into large vessel. ADD Decaf and stir till dissolved. Serve over ice in tall glasses. Pass sugar and cream, if desired.	4½ qts.	2-oz. jar
45	POUR into large vessel .... ADD Decaf and stir till dissolved. STIR in additional water .... Serve over ice in tall glasses. (Mixture will be foamy on top, at first.) Pass sugar and cream, if desired.	1 qt. 10¼ qts.	5-oz. jar

Cocoa — The Universal Flavor

RICH HOT CHOCOLATE

COMBINE in top of double boiler
 1 6-oz. pkg. (1 c.) Semi-Sweet Chocolate Morsels
 1 c. water
 Dash salt

Place over moderate heat till semi-sweet melts, then stir till well blended

Bring to a boil, stirring constantly

Place over boiling water

ADD
 1½ c. heavy cream
 1½ c. milk

Heat to scalding

Beat with rotary beater till foamy

Serve at once

YIELD: 6 servings

(continued on page 176)

(continued from page 175)

Variations:

1. Serve, if desired, with topping of whipped cream, sprinkled with grated orange rind
2. Place mint wafer in bottom of each cup before filling with Hot Chocolate

Remember that for *perfect beginnings,* too, a perfectly nourished, perfectly wonderful day starts with a cup of hot cocoa for breakfast.
(See illustration 24)

HOT NESTLÉ'S EVERREADY COCOA

GROUP SERVINGS

SERVINGS	DIRECTIONS	BOILING WATER*	AMOUNTS OF EVERREADY
1	PLACE EverReady in cup. ADD boiling water and stir.	6 oz.	3 heaping tsp.
6	PLACE EverReady in small vessel. STIR in boiling water, slowly.	1 qt.	1½ c.
16	PLACE EverReady in large vessel. STIR in boiling water, slowly.	2½ qts.	1-lb. can
32	PLACE EverReady in large vessel. STIR in boiling water, slowly.	5 qts.	2-lb. Family-Size can

*To provide extra nourishment for growing children, use hot milk.

Tea – The Cup That Cheers

For the majority of the world, tea is the daily beverage, whether it's taken from glasses, thin china cups, or pottery mugs. In America, too, we love tea, hot and cold, and afternoon tea can be a most pleasant facet of life in our hurry-hurry schedules.

But iced tea is particularly American, the great warm-weather drink for young and old. Using Nestea®, iced tea is one of the simplest things to enjoy wherever you are. Have it as your fancy dictates; choose any of these trims to make this delightful drink more delightful still.

ICED TEA TRIMS

LEMON WHEEL: Cut lemon slice nearly to center; draw stem of mint sprig through cut; slip over rim of glass

BERRY SENTRY: Press large strawberry, point down, over rim; tuck mint sprig into glass

OAHU FLAGS: Cut stick of fresh pineapple (2¾" x ¾" x ½"). Toothpick watercress sprig and drained maraschino cherry to side. Cut pineapple stick from bottom to toothpick; slip over rim of glass

FLYING CARTWHEELS: Cut 2½" round from ¾" slice of watermelon. Slit round nearly to center. Tuck mint sprigs through slit from each side. Slip over rim of glass

ORANGE AIDS: Cut wedge from unpeeled orange. Toothpick watercress sprig and kumquat to rind side. Slit rind from point to toothpick. Slip over rim of glass, rind-side out

HIGH MOON: Cut small wedge from unpeeled cantaloupe. Toothpick watermelon ball to inside of wedge. Slit cantaloupe from point to toothpick. Slip over rim of glass, rind-side in. Press mint sprig into iced tea

SUGAR-FROSTED GLASSES: Frost rim of glass by dipping first in very slightly beaten egg white, then in tinted and flavored sugar. Let stand till dry before filling glass. For thicker coating, repeat dipping

To tint and flavor sugar: Add few drops of food coloring and desired flavoring extract to small amount of sugar; blend well with fork. Dry and place in small bowl, to make deeper "collar" on glass

FANCY ICE CUBES: In each section of ice-cube tray, place: Small mint sprig *or* quarter slice of lime or lemon *or* maraschino cherry *or* strawberry. Add a little water; freeze. Fill tray with water; freeze.

HOT TEA TODDY

COMBINE and let steep 5 min.
   3 c. boiling water
   4 rounded tsp. Nestea

HEAT *just* to boiling
   1 6-oz. can frozen lemonade concentrate

ADD to
   Hot Nestea
Pour into heated cups

ADD
   1 1" strip lemon peel and sprinkle with Nutmeg

YIELD: 4 servings
(See illustration 5)

page 178 | *beverages*

PIQUANT MULLED TEA

COMBINE in saucepan and boil 5 min.
- ½ c. honey
- ½ c. water
- 1½ tsp. grated orange rind
- 1 tsp. grated lemon rind
- 1 2″ stick cinnamon

Turn heat to low

ADD and keep hot
- ¼ c. orange juice
- ¼ c. pineapple juice
- 2 tbs. lemon juice

COMBINE and let steep 5 min.
- 6 c. boiling water
- 3 tbs. Nestea

ADD to
- Fruit mixture

Serve hot in heated pottery cups or mugs

> **YIELD:** approx. 10 servings
> *(See illustration 28)*

STRAWBERRY TEA

POUR into 8-cup teapot
- 1½ qts. boiling water

ADD and mix well
- ¾ c. Nestlé's Strawberry Quik
- 6 tbs. Nestea
- 3 tbs. lemon juice
- ¼ tsp. whole cloves

Serve hot

> **YIELD:** 8 servings

HOT TEA PUNCH

COMBINE; cover and steep for 5 min.
- 1 qt. boiling water
- 1 c. orange juice
- 1 6-oz. can frozen limeade concentrate, thawed
- 4 tsp. Nestea
- 1 2″ stick cinnamon
- ½ tsp. whole cloves

Strain into large heat-resistant bowl

STIR in
- 2 c. boiling water
- 1 c. pineapple juice

Serve hot

> **YIELD:** approx. 16 servings
> *(See illustration 2)*

GOLDEN WEDDING PUNCH

COMBINE in 2-qt. container and stir briskly
- 2 c. water
- 2 rounded tbs. Nestea

ADD and stir to dissolve sugar
- 3 c. orange juice
- 1 c. lemon juice
- 1 c. pineapple juice
- ½ c. sugar
- ¼ c. grenadine

Chill

PLACE in punch bowl
- Large block of ice

POUR over ice
- Nestea mixture
- 1 28-oz. bottle ginger ale

GARNISH with
- Slices of fresh pineapple, cut in bell shapes
- Large fresh strawberries, cut in halves, lengthwise

> **YIELD:** 22 4-oz. servings

SHERRIED TEA FLIP
COMBINE
- ¼ c. Nestea
- ¼ c. sugar
- ⅛ tsp. cinnamon
- Dash mace

ADD and stir briskly
- 3 c. cold tap water

BEAT in till smooth and frothy
- 1 pt. softened vanilla ice cream
- ¾ c. cream sherry

Pour in tall glasses

YIELD: 4 servings

TOKAY CORDIAL
COMBINE and let stand 1 hr.
- Contents of one 10-oz. pkg. frozen, sliced strawberries
- 1½ c. white Tokay wine

POUR into large pitcher
- 1 qt. cold tap water

ADD and stir briskly
- 5 tbs. Nestea
- 5 tbs. sugar

ADD
- Strawberry-Tokay mixture

PLACE in punch bowl
- Large block of ice

POUR over
- Nestea mixture

Garnish with lime twists or fresh mint leaves, if desired

YIELD: approx. 12 servings

RASPBERRY SHRUB
COMBINE in large pitcher and stir till dissolved
- 6½ c. cold tap water
- ½ c. sugar
- ⅓ c. Nestea

ADD
- 1 10-oz. pkg. frozen raspberries, thawed
- 1 c. orange juice
- 1 c. lemon juice

Chill several hours or overnight

To serve:

PLACE in each of ten 10-oz. glasses
- 2 oz. cracked ice (approx. 2 cubes)

FILL with
- Nestea mixture

YIELD: 10 servings
(See illustration 22)

HONEYED ORANGE COOLER
COMBINE in tall glass and stir briskly
- 1 tbs. Nestea
- 2 tbs. cold water

STIR in
- 2 tsp. frozen orange juice concentrate
- 1 tsp. honey
- Cold water to fill glass

YIELD: 1 serving
(See illustration 21)

page 179 | beverages

page 180 | *beverages*

TEA GARDEN BRACER

COMBINE and boil 5 min.
¾ c. sugar
¾ c. water
1 tsp. whole allspice
1 2″ stick cinnamon

COMBINE and add
¼ c. *actively* boiling water
8 rounded tsp. Nestea
Cover and let stand 10 min. Strain

ADD
2 qts. iced water
¾ c. orange juice
½ c. lemon juice

To serve:

PLACE in each of eight 10-oz. glasses
2 oz. cracked ice
(approx. 2 cubes)

FILL with
Nestea mixture

YIELD: 8 servings

PINEAPPLE TEA COOLER

COMBINE in old fashioned glass
(8-oz.) and stir briskly
¼ c. cold tap water
2 tbs. pineapple syrup*
1 tsp. Nestea

ADD
2 to 3 ice cubes
1 slice canned pineapple,
cut in half

*Use syrup from canned pineapple

SPARKLING TEA 'N' SHERBET COOLER

COMBINE in tall glass and stir briskly
1 tbs. Nestea
1 tbs. sugar
Small amount cold tap water

ADD
1 scoop softened orange or lemon
sherbet (approx. ½ c.)

FILL slowly with
Chilled sparkling water

YIELD: 1 serving

NESTEA FRUIT SHRUB

COMBINE in 2½-qt. container
and stir briskly
8 tsp. Nestea
6½ c. cold water

STIR in
1 10-oz. pkg. frozen
strawberries, thawed
1 6-oz. can frozen limeade,
thawed

Serve at once

YIELD: 10 to 12 servings

NESTEA

GROUP SERVINGS

SERVINGS	DIRECTIONS	BOILING WATER	NESTEA
HOT NESTEA			
Single	PLACE Nestea in cup. ADD boiling water and stir.	5-oz.	1 level tsp.
42	PLACE Nestea in large vessel. ADD boiling water and stir.	7½ qts.	¾-oz. jar
84	PLACE Nestea in large vessel. ADD boiling water and stir.	15 qts. (3¾ gals.)	1½-oz. jar
ICED NESTEA		COLD TAP WATER	NESTEA
Single	Fill tall glass with cold water. ADD Nestea and stir. ADD ice, sugar and lemon to taste.	8-oz.	1 rounded tsp.
30	PLACE Nestea in large vessel. ADD cold water and stir briskly. Pour over ice in tall glasses. Serve with sugar and lemon to taste.	7½ qts.	¾-oz. jar
60	PLACE Nestea in large vessel. ADD cold water and stir briskly. Pour over ice in tall glasses. Serve with sugar and lemon to taste.	15 qts. (3¾ gals.)	1½-oz. jar

More Hot and Cold Refreshers

STRAWBERRY SPARKLER

COMBINE in large bowl or pitcher
 4 c. water
 ¾ c. sugar
 ½ c. Nestlé's Strawberry Quik
Stir till sugar and Quik are dissolved

ADD
 ½ c. drained, crushed pineapple
 ½ c. lemon juice
 ½ c. orange juice

Serve with ice in frosted glasses (Dip rims in ½" lemon juice and dust with sugar. Let stand to dry before using).

YIELD: 4 to 6 servings

(See illustration 27)

page 182 | beverages

PINK ELEPHANT PUNCH

BLEND together in a 3-qt. bowl
3 ripe bananas, mashed
1 c. Nestlé's Strawberry Quik

STIR in gradually
1 qt. milk

SCOOP on top and stir till ice cream is partially melted
1 qt. vanilla ice cream

YIELD: 12 servings

PINK PARTY PUNCH

COMBINE in bowl
5½ c. cold water
1 6-oz. can frozen lemonade concentrate
½ c. Nestlé's Strawberry Quik

PLACE in a punch bowl
1 qt. vanilla ice cream
1 pt. pineapple sherbet

Break into small pieces, using a large spoon

ADD
Quik mixture

Stir till ice cream and sherbet are partially melted

Serve at once in punch cups

YIELD: approx. 20 servings
(See illustration 26)

MINTY WAY

COMBINE in covered 1½-qt. refrigerator container, and stir to blend
4 c. milk
8 heaping tsp. Nestlé's Chocolate Quik
¼ tsp. peppermint extract

Cover and chill

Shake well before serving

YIELD: 4 servings
(See illustration 25)

CALYPSO SHAKE

COMBINE in covered 1½-qt. refrigerator container, and stir to blend
4 c. milk
8 heaping tsp. Nestlé's Chocolate Quik
2 ripe bananas, finely mashed

Cover and chill

Shake well before serving

YIELD: 4 servings
(See illustration 22)

STRAWBERRY FLIP

COMBINE
2½ c. cold water
¾ c. Nestlé's Strawberry Quik
3 tbs. lemon juice

Pour over shaved ice

GARNISH with
Mint sprigs

YIELD: 4 servings
(See illustration 22)

CREAMY QUIK NOG

BEAT till stiff but not dry
  1 egg white

BEAT in gradually till stiff and glossy
  2 tbs. sugar

BEAT together
  1¼ c. milk
  ⅓ c. Nestlé's Chocolate Quik
  1 egg yolk

BLEND in
  ½ c. heavy cream, whipped
  Egg white mixture
  ⅛ tsp. orange extract

Pour in tall glasses

YIELD: 3 servings

HOT QUIK NOG

COMBINE and beat till very thick
  2 eggs
  ¼ c. sugar

COMBINE and bring *just* to boil
  2 c. milk
  ½ c. Nestlé's Chocolate Quik

ADD slowly to egg mixture, stirring rapidly
  Hot Quik mixture

Cook over moderate heat 2 min., stirring constantly

Pour in cups

Sprinkle with cinnamon or nutmeg (optional)

YIELD: 4 servings

Note: This may be made in advance; chilled, and reheated over moderate heat, stirring constantly. Remove from heat and beat till foamy —approx. 1 min.

INDIVIDUAL QUIK EGG NOG

COMBINE in tall glass and beat briskly with fork till smooth
  2 heaping tsp. Nestlé's Chocolate Quik
  Small amount of milk
  1 egg

FILL with
  Cold milk

TOP with
  Whipped cream (optional)
  Nutmeg

YIELD: 1 serving

QUIK 'N' PEANUT

COMBINE in saucepan
  1½ c. milk
  ¼ c. Nestlé's Chocolate Quik
  1 tbs. cream-style peanut butter
  1 tbs. sugar

Bring *just* to boil over moderate heat, stirring constantly

Remove from heat and beat well

Pour in cups

TOP with
  Whipped cream

YIELD: 2 servings

page 184 / beverages

CREAMY QUIK

COMBINE in tall glass and stir briskly till smooth

3 heaping tsp. Nestlé's Chocolate Quik

1 heaping tbs. marshmallow cream

Small amount of milk

STIR in till blended

Cold milk to fill glass

QUIK MILKY FIZZER

POUR into tall glass

¾ c. milk

STIR in

1 tbs. honey*

2 heaping tsp. Nestlé's Chocolate Quik

FILL with

Chilled sparkling water

Stir quickly till foamy

YIELD: 1 serving

*OR substitute 1 tablespoon maple-blended syrup or 1 tablespoon light molasses

HOT CINNAMON QUIK

COMBINE in saucepan and bring *just* to boil over moderate heat, stirring constantly

1 c. milk*

3 heaping tsp. Nestlé's Chocolate Quik

⅛ tsp. cinnamon

*Water may be substituted for milk

NESTLÉ'S CHOCOLATE AND STRAWBERRY QUIK

GROUP SERVINGS

SERVINGS	DIRECTIONS	COLD MILK	AMOUNTS OF CHOCOLATE OR STRAWBERRY QUIK
Single	POUR milk in tall glass. ADD Quik and stir briskly.	8 ozs.	2 heaping tsp.
21	EMPTY Quik into large vessel. ADD and stir till smooth .... STIR in additional	½ c. 5 qts.	1-lb. can
54	EMPTY Quik into large vessel. ADD and stir till smooth .... STIR in additional	1½ c. 3 gals.	2-lb. 6-oz. can (Family Size— available only in Chocolate)

Index

A la Mode Sandwiches, 164
Alaskan Pie, Layered, 100
Angel Food Hidden Treasure Cake, 29
Angel Food Tunnel of Love Cake, 29
Applesauce Loaf Cake, 17
Applesauce Pie, 98
Arabian Coffee, 172
Arabian Delights (cookies), 66
Australian Coffee Foam, 172
Australian Squares, 71

Baked Alaska (Layered Alaskan Pie), 100
Banana Bars, Jamaica, 69
Banana Kabobs, Frozen, 163
Barbecue Sweetwiches, 107
Bavarian Mint Pie, 97
Beau Catchers (cookies), 57-58

BEVERAGES
 see also Cocoa, Coffee, Milk Shakes, Punch, Sodas, Tea
 Australian Coffee Foam, 172
 Calypso Shake, 182
 Cocoa, 176
 Coffee Banana Cooler, 170
 Coffee Coolers, 169
 Coffee Mallow Smoothie, 171
 Creamy Café Float, 173
 Creamy Quik, 184
 Creamy Quik Nog, 183
 Decaf, 175
 Gold Coast Gaiety, 170
 Hawaiian Coolers, 170
 Honeyed Orange Cooler, 179
 Hot Cinnamon Quik, 184
 Hot Quik Nog, 183
 Hot Tea Toddy, 177
 Individual Quik Egg Nog, 183
 Minty Way, 182
 Mocha Dilly, 172
 Nescafé, 174
 Nestea, 181
 Nestea Fruit Shrub, 180
 Pineapple Tea Cooler, 180
 Piquant Mulled Tea, 178
 Quik Milky Fizzer, 184
 Quik 'n' Peanut, 183
 Raspberry Shrub, 179
 Rich Hot Chocolate, 175-176
 Sherried Tea Flip, 179
 Sparkling Tea 'n' Sherbet Cooler, 180
 Strawberry Flip, 182
 Strawberry Sparkler, 181
 Strawberry Tea, 178
 Tea Garden Bracer, 180
 Tokay Cordial, 179
 West Indian Juleps, 171

Black Bottom Pie, 89
Bon Bon Fudge, 142
Bon Bon Tea Cakes, 54
Bourbon Balls, 144
Brown Cow (soda), 164
Brown Orchid Soufflé, 125
Brown Velvet Cake, 14
Brownie Pie, 92
Brownies, "Easy-to-Make" Deluxe, 72
Brownies, Fudge, 41
Brownies, Nut Mallow, 41
Brûlot Nescafé, 171
Butter-Choc Frosting, 26
Butterchocs (candy), 139
Butterscotch Apple Crisp, 110
Butterscotch Apples, 142
Butterscotch Butter Frosting, 24
Butterscotch Chiffon Pie, 95
Butterscotch Chiffon Pie, Café, 94
Butterscotch Coconut Drops (cookies), 81
Butterscotch-Cream Cheese Frosting, 24
Butterscotch Cream Fudge, 137
Butterscotch Crispie Squares (candy), 139
Butterscotch Delight Frosting, 24
Butterscotch Delight Layer Cake, 18
Butterscotch Frosting, Creamy, 24
Butterscotch Fudge, Easy, 137
Butterscotch Nut Squares (cookies), 46
Butterscotch Oatmeal Crisps, 82
Butterscotch Peanut Crisps (candy), 139
Butterscotch-Peanut Banana Pops, 163
Butterscotch-Peanut Butter Fudge, 137
Butterscotch Pecan Pie, Deep South, 94
Butterscotch Pralines, 138
Butterscotch Raisin Bars, 45
Butterscotch Sauce, 132
Butterscotch Scotchies (cookies), 45
Butterscotch Snaps, 81

page 186 | *index*

Butterscotch Sundae Sauce, 167
Butterscotch Thins, 56
Butterscotch Toffee Topper Bars, 44

Café au Lait, 170
Café Butterscotch Chiffon Pie, 94
Café Cacao, 173
Café Cacao Frappé, 173
Café Caribe, 173
Café Float, Creamy, 173
Café Pumpkin Pie, 101
Café Cointreau for Two, 170
Cake Decorating, Fillings, Frostings,
   Glazes, Sauces and Toppings:
   see Index

CAKES

Applesauce Loaf, 17
Brown Velvet, 14
Butterscotch Delight Layers, 18
Calico Crumb, 17
Carol Cake, 28
Choco-Date, 11
Chocolate Layer, 15
Chocolate Pecan Crumb, 13
Chocolate Upside Down Cake, 15
Coconut Marble Fudge, 20
Dark Secret Pound, 14
Devil's Delight, 9
Devil's Food, 10
Double Marble, 11
Frozen Cream Chiffon Roll, 150
Glossy Chocolate Squares, 12
Hawaiian Pineapple, 18
Hidden Treasure, 29
Holiday Fruit, 16
Luxury Loaf, 13
Mahogany Fudge, 12
Mardi Gras Party, 19
Mocha Nut Torte, 123
New Orleans Torte, 124
Party Butterfly, 16
Party Chocolate Cheese Cake, 121
Strawberry Dessert Roll, 105
Swiss Chocolate, 10
Tunnel of Love, 29

Calico Crumb Cake, 17
Calico Squares, October, 46
Calypso Shake, 182
Candied Fruit Topping, 129

CANDIES

Bon Bon Fudge, 142
Bourbon Balls, 144
Butterchocs, 139
Butterscotch Apples, 142
Butterscotch Cream Fudge, 137

Butterscotch Crispie Squares, 139
Butterscotch-Peanut Butter Fudge,
   137
Butterscotch Peanut Crisps, 139
Butterscotch Pralines, 138
Cobblestone Candy, 146
Chocolate Almond Brittle, 143
Chocolate-Caramel Pecan Drops, 144
Chocolate Fudgies, 136
Chocolate King Mallows, 145
Chocolate Quickies, 140
Easy Butterscotch Fudge, 137
Easy Creamy Fudge, 135
EverReady Campers' Fudge, 136
Hopscotchers, 139
Lollipop Marshmallows, 140
Marshmallow Cream Fudge, 138
Mocha Coconut Patties, 141
Nescafé Glazed Pecans, 143
Peanut Butter King Mallows, 146
Quik Fudgies, 136
Ribbon Candies, 143
Scotch Crispies, 138
Scrabble Squares, 141
Short Cut Fudge, 135
Strawberry Crispies, 140
Strawberry Fruit Balls, 144
Sugar Plum Trees, 145
Two-Tone Mallow Bites, 146
Walnut Chocolettes, 141

Candy Bar Cookies, 48
Carol Cake, 28
Cheese Cake, Party Chocolate, 121
Cheese Pie, Heavenly, 99
Chewy Honey Sticks, 48
Chiffon Roll, Frozen Cream, 150
Choc-Oat Crisps, 52
Choco-Berry Fizz, 165
Choco-Date Cake, 11
Choco-Orange Oaties, 87
Chocolat de Brazil Mousse, 124
Chocolat, Mousse au, 123
Chocolat, Soufflé, au Froid, 126
Chocolat, Soufflé Bain Marie, 125
Chocolate Almond Brittle, 143
Chocolate Almond Pie, 92
Chocolate Almond Teas (cookies), 63
Chocolate Banana Cookies, 86
Chocolate Bavarian, "Laced," 107
Chocolate Butter-Cream Filling, 25
Chocolate Butter Frosting, 23
Chocolate-Caramel Pecan Drops, 144
Chocolate Charlotte Russe, 106
Chocolate Cheese Cake, Party, 121
Chocolate Cracklers (cookies), 60
Chocolate Cream Crown, 28
Chocolate Cream Cups, 110

Chocolate Cream Frosting, 22
Chocolate Crisps, 86
Chocolate Crunchy Sandwich Cookies, 85
Chocolate Dessert Pancakes, 126
Chocolate Dessert Waffles, 127
Chocolate Dips, 132
Chocolate Filling and Glaze, 21
Chocolate Fondant Glaze, 22
Chocolate Frosteds (cookies), 55
Chocolate Frosting, Easy, 22
Chocolate Frosting, Easy EverReady, 23
Chocolate Frosting, Glossy, 23
Chocolate Frosting, Luscious, 21
Chocolate Frosting, Speedy, 21
Chocolate Fudgies, 136
Chocolate Graham Loaf, 152
Chocolate Heavenly Crown, 122
Chocolate Ice Cream, 149
Chocolate Igloos, 149
Chocolate King Mallows, 145
Chocolate Layer Cake, 15
Chocolate Lebkuchen, 65
Chocolate Marshmallow Sauce, 131
Chocolate Mousse, Frozen, 152
Chocolate-Nut Mosaics (cookies), 54
Chocolate-Oat Sugar Balls, 62
Chocolate Peanut Butter Oat Cookies, 84
Chocolate-Peanut Sauce, 129
Chocolate Pecan Crumb Cake, 13
Chocolate Pecan Pie, 91
Chocolate Peppermint Creams (cookies), 62
Chocolate Pie, Delicious, 89
Chocolate Pops, 162
Chocolate Pops, DeLuxe, 162
Chocolate Puddin' Cake, 111
Chocolate Puffs, Frozen, 151
Chocolate Quickies (candy), 140
Chocolate Quik, 184
Chocolate Quik Pudding, 3-Minute, 105
Chocolate Quik Sauce, 133
Chocolate Quik Soda, 164
Chocolate Refrigerator Cookies, 52
Chocolate-Rice Pie, Fluffy, 90
Chocolate Sauce, Creamy, 130
Chocolate Sauce, Olympia, 130
Chocolate Sauce, Thin, 166
Chocolate Shadow Glaze, 29
Chocolate Silhouettes, Festive, 27
Chocolate Soufflé Cups, 122
Chocolate Sour Cream Velvet Frosting, 25
Chocolate Squares, Glossy, 12
Chocolate Sugar-Pecan Bars, 51
Chocolate Upside Down Cake, 15
Chocolate Velvet (pudding), 106
Chocolate Velvet Frosting, 22
Choco-Nut Delight Bars, 43
Choco-Nut Dream Bars, 42
Choco-Nut Whizzers (cookies), 83
Choco-Orange Oaties, 87
Choco-Pineapple Frosties, 150
Christmas Candy, 142-147
Christmas Cookies, 57-63
Cobblestone Candy, 146

COCOA

Cocoa, 176
EverReady, 176
Rich Hot Chocolate, 175-176
for cocoa-flavored drinks, see Beverages

Cocoa Cream Frosting, 23
Cocoa Mallow Sundae Sauce, 166
Coconut Marble Fudge Cake, 20

COFFEE

Arabian Coffee, 172
Brûlot Nescafé, 171
Café au Lait, 170
Café Cacao, 173
Café Cacao Frappé, 173
Café Caribe, 173
Café Cointreau for Two, 170
Coolers, 169
Creamy Nescafé, 170
Decaf, 175
Honeypot Coffee, 170
Nescafé, 174
Syrian Coffee, 172
for coffee-flavored drinks, see Beverages

Coffee Banana Cooler, 170
Coffee Foam, Australian, 172
Coffee Hard Sauce, 131
Coffee Mallow Smoothie (beverage), 171
Coffee Milk Shake, 165
Coffee Sauce, Speedy, 166
Coffee Sundae Sauce, 167
Coffee-Toffee Bars, 47

COOKIES

Bar
Australian Squares, 71
Butterscotch Nut Squares, 46
Butterscotch Raisin Bars, 45
Butterscotch Scotchies, 45
Butterscotch Toffee Toppers, 44
Candy Bar Cookies, 48
Chewy Honey Sticks, 48
Chocolate Lebkuchen, 65
Chocolate Sugar-Pecan Bars, 51

page 188 | *index*

Choco-Nut Delights, 43
Choco-Nut Dream Bars, 42
Coffee-Toffee Bars, 47
Crispie Fudge Bars, 50
Crunchy Fudge Bars, 44
Double-Scotch Pecan Bars, 49
Easy Polka Dot Squares, 43
"Easy-to-Make" DeLuxe
Brownies, 72
"Easy-to-Make" Toll House Marble
Squares, 32
Fudge Brownies, 41
Jamaica Banana Bars, 69
Jumbo Bars, 53
Near East Date-Orange Bars, 70
Nut Mallow Brownies, 41
October Calico Squares, 46
Oriental Brittle "Cookies," 66
Petits Four Squares, 50
Polka Dot Squares, 42
Quick Party Bars, 49
Sandwich Crunch Bars, 47
Three-Tone Party Squares, 51
Toll House Marble Squares, 32

Drop

Arabian Delights, 66
Beau Catchers, 57-58
Bon Bon Tea Cakes, 54
Butterscotch Coconut Drops, 81
Butterscotch Oatmeal Crisps, 82
Butterscotch Snaps, 81
Chocolate Almond Teas, 63
Chocolate Banana Cookies, 86
Chocolate Cracklers, 60
Chocolate Crisps, 86
Chocolate Frosteds, 55
Chocolate-Oat Sugar Balls, 62
Chocolate Peanut Butter Oat, 84
Chocolate Peppermint Creams, 62
Choco-Nut Whizzers, 83
Choco-Orange Oaties, 87
Corn Flake Meringoons, 85
Crinkly Puffs, 84
Crunchy Sandwich Cookies, 85
"Easy-to-Make" Drop Cookies, 72
Festive Clusters, 58
Florentine Dainties, 59
French Chocolate Meringues, 67
Harlequin Dippers, 55
Holland Snaps, 71
Lacy English Jumbos, 66
Latin American Cookies, 70
Meringue Surprises, 84
Mincemeat Jumbles, 61
Mocha Pecan Buttons, 86
Molasses Dandies, 83

Original Toll House Cookies, 31
Peekaboo Bon Bons, 60
Polka Dot Platters, 61
Sand Tarts, 63
Sandies, 63
Scandinavian Snappers, 65
Scotch-Oat Prizes, 82
Strawberry Kisses, 83
Swiss Chews, 68
Swiss Fruit-Nut, 64
Toll House Variations, 31-32
Viennese, 64

Refrigerator

Butterscotch Thins, 56
Choc-Oat Crisps, 52
Chocolate, 52
Chocolate-Nut Mosaics, 54
Date Butterscotch, 56
Irish Whirligigs, 68
Jumbo Bars, 53
Swedish Delicacies, 67

Rolled

Candy Bar Cookies, 48
Irish Whirligigs, 68
Strawberry, 87

Corn Flake Meringoons, 85

CREAM PUFFS

Croquembouche, 112
Frozen Chocolate Puffs, 151
Petits Puffs, Café, 105

Croquembouche, 112
Crumb Cake, Calico, 17
Crumb Cake, Chocolate Pecan, 13
Cupcakes, Party Butterfly, 16
Cupcakes, Devil's Delight, 9

Dark Magic Sauce, 131
Dark Secret Pound Cake, 14
Date Butterscotch Cookies, 56
Date-Orange Bars, Near East, 70
Decaf, 175
Decorating Cakes, 27-29
Decorating Cookies, 87
Dessert Doughnut Log, 128
Devil's Delight Cake, 9
Devil's Food Cake, 10
Double Marble Cake, 11
Double-Scotch Pecan Bars, 49

DOUGHNUT DESSERTS

À la Mode Sandwiches, 164
Dessert Log, 128
Meringue Cups, 127
Two-Tone Doughnut Crumble, 127

Drop Cookies, "Easy-to-Make," 72

Easy-Do Pie, 93
Egg Nog, Creamy Quik, 183
Egg Nog, Hot Quik, 183
Egg Nog, Individual Quik, 183
EverReady Cocoa, 176
EverReady Frosting, Easy, 23
EverReady Sundae Sauce, 167

Festive Clusters (cookies), 58
Florentine Dainties (cookies), 59
Foreign Cookies, 64-71

FILLINGS
Chocolate, 21
Chocolate Butter-Cream, 25
Chocolate Cream Crown, 28
Hidden Treasure, 29
Tunnel of Love, 29

French Chocolate Meringues, 67
French Mocha Ice Cream, 151

FROSTINGS
Butter-Choc, 26
Butterscotch Butter, 24
Butterscotch-Cream Cheese, 24
Butterscotch Delight, 24
Chocolate Butter, 23
Chocolate Cream, 22
Chocolate Cream Crown, 28
Chocolate Velvet, 22
Cocoa Cream, 23
Creamy Butterscotch, 24
Easy Chocolate, 22
Easy EverReady, 23
Fluffy Marble, 25
Fluffy Strawberry, 26
Fudge, 25
Glossy Chocolate, 23
Luscious Chocolate, 21
Quik Chocolate, 23
Sour Cream Velvet, 25
Speedy Chocolate, 21
Strawberry Butter, 26
Strawberry Whipped Cream, 132

FROZEN DESSERTS
À la Mode Sandwiches, 164
Butterscotch-Peanut Banana Pops, 163
Chocolate Graham Loaf, 152
Chocolate Ice Cream, 149
Chocolate Igloos, 149
Chocolate Pops, 162
Choco-Pineapple Frosties, 150
Deluxe Chocolate Pops, 162
Deluxe Strawberry Pops, 163
French Mocha Ice Cream, 151
Frozen Banana Kabobs, 163
Frozen Chocolate Mousse, 152
Frozen Chocolate Puffs, 151
Frozen Cream Chiffon Roll, 150
Frozen Strawberry Mousse, 152
Layered Alaskan Pie, 100
Mocha Delight Freeze, 151
Nescafé Tortoni, 149
Orange "Chip" Dessert, 161
Orange-Chocolate Mousse, 161
Quik Covered Pops, 162
Strawberry-Pineapple Parfait, 163

Fruit Cake, Holiday, 16
Fruity Quik Milk "Shake," 165

FUDGE
Bon Bon, 142
Butterscotch Cream, 137
Butterscotch-Peanut Butter, 137
Chocolate Fudgies, 136
Easy Butterscotch, 137
Easy Creamy, 135
EverReady Campers', 136
Marshmallow Cream, 138
Quik Fudgies, 136
Short Cut, 135

Fudge Bars, Crispie, 50
Fudge Bars, Crunchy, 44
Fudge Brownies, 41
Fudge Cake, Mahogany, 12
Fudge Frosting, 25
Fudge Sauce, Hot, 131
Fudge Sauce, Speedy, 130
Fudge Sundae Sauce, 167

Gala Pie, 103
Glazed Pecans, Nescafé, 143

GLAZES
Carol Cake, 28
Chocolate, 21
Chocolate Fondant, 22
Chocolate Shadow, 29
Festive Chocolate Silhouettes, 27

Gold Coast Chiffon Pie, 96
Gold Coast Gaiety (beverage), 170
Golden Wedding Punch, 178
Graham Cracker Barbecue Sweetwiches, 107
Graham Cracker Napoleonettes, 108
Graham Cracker Stackmores, 109

Harlequin Dippers, 55
Hawaiian Coolers, 170

page 190 | index

Hawaiian Pineapple Cake for a Crowd, 18
Holland Snaps, 71
Honey Peanut Butter Topping, 129
Honey Sticks, Chewy, 48
Honeyed Orange Cooler, 179
Honeypot Coffee, 170
Hopscotchers (candy), 139
Hot Chocolate, Rich, 175-176
Hot Tea Punch, 178
Hot Tea Toddy, 177

ICE CREAM

Chocolate, 149
Chocolate Igloos, 149
French Mocha, 151
Mocha Delight Freeze, 151
Nescafé Tortoni, 149
Ice Cream Sauces: *see Sauces, Sundae and Sauces and Toppings*
Iced Tea Trims, 177
Instant Pudding Parfait, 109
Irish Whirligigs (cookies), 68

Jamaica Banana Bars, 69
Jumbo Bars, 53

Lacy English Jumbos (cookies), 66
Latin American Cookies, 70
Layered Alaskan Pie, 100
Lebkuchen, Chocolate, 65
Loaf Cake, Luxury, 13
Lollipop Marshmallows, 140

Marble Cake, Double, 11
Marble Delight Pie, 98
Marble Frosting, Fluffy, 25
Marble Squares, Toll House, 32
Mardi Gras Party Cake, 19
Marshmallow Cream Fudge, 138
Mediterranean Pie, 99
Meringue Doughnut Cups, 127
Meringue Surprises (cookies), 84
Meringues, French Chocolate, 67
Meringues, Strawberry Kisses, 83

MILK SHAKES

Calypso Shake, 182
Coffee Milk Shake, 165
Fruity Quik Milk "Shake," 165
Minty Way, 182
Strawberry Double-Frosted, 165

Mincemeat Jumbles, 61
Minted Float (dessert), 111
Minty Way (milk shake), 182
Mocha Angel Pie, 90
Mocha Bavarian, 121
Mocha Bisque Pie, 91
Mocha Coconut Patties (candy), 141
Mocha Cream Pie, 93
Mocha Delight Freeze, 151
Mocha Dilly, 172
Mocha Nut Torte, 123
Mocha Pecan Buttons (cookies), 86
Molasses Dandies (cookies), 83

MOUSSE

au Chocolat, 123
Chocolat de Brazil, 124
Frozen Chocolate, 152
Frozen Strawberry, 152
Orange-Chocolate, 161
Mulled Tea, Piquant, 178

Namesake Cookies, 87
Napoleonettes, 108
Nescafé, 174
Nescafé Cream Pie, 96
Nescafé, Creamy, 170
Nescafé Glazed Pecans, 143
Nescafé Soda, 164
Nescafé Tortoni, 149
Nesselrode Pie, Easy, 101
Nestea, 181
Nestea Fruit Shrub, 180
New Orleans Torte, 124
Nut Mallow Brownies, 41

One, Two, Three Sauce, 128
Orange "Chip" Dessert, 161
Orange-Chocolate Mousse, 161
Orange Cream Pie, 95
Orange Marmalade Topping, 129
Oriental Brittle "Cookies," 66
Original Toll House Cookies, 31

Pancake Nescafé Sauce, 133

PANCAKES, DESSERT

Chocolate, 126
Strawberry, 128

PARFAITS

Instant Pudding Parfait, 109
Parfait Parisienne, 109
Strawberry-Pineapple, 163

Party Butterfly Cakes, 16
Party Squares, Three-Tone, 51
Peach Carousel Pie, 102
Peach Crisp, 108
Peanut Butter King Mallows, 146
Pecan Bars, Double-Scotch, 49
Pecan Buttons, Mocha, 86
Pecan Pie, Butterscotch, 94
Pecan Pie, Chocolate, 91
Pecans, Nescafé Glazed, 143
Peekaboo Bob Bons (cookies), 60
Petits Four Squares, 50
Petits Puff Café, 105

PIES

    Applesauce Pie, 98
    Bavarian Mint, 97
    Black Bottom, 89
    Brownie, 92
    Butterscotch Chiffon, 95
    Café Butterscotch Chiffon, 94
    Café Pumpkin, 101
    Chocolate Almond, 92
    Chocolate Pecan, 91
    Deep South Butterscotch Pecan, 94
    Delicious Chocolate, 89
    Easy-Do, 93
    Easy Nesselrode, 101
    Fluffy Chocolate-Rice, 90
    Gala, 103
    Gold Coast Chiffon, 96
    Heavenly Cheese, 99
    Layered Alaskan, 100
    Marble Delight, 98
    Mediterranean, 99
    Mocha Angel, 90
    Mocha Bisque, 91
    Mocha Cream, 93
    Nescafé Cream, 96
    Orange Cream, 95
    Peach Carousel, 102
    Triple Treat, 102

Pineapple Butterscotch Sauce, 129
Pineapple Cake, Hawaiian, 18
Pineapple Tea Cooler, 180
Pink Elephant Punch, 182
Pink Party Punch, 182
Polka Dot Platters (cookies), 61
Polka Dot Squares, 42
Polka Dot Squares, Easy, 43

POPS, FROZEN

    Butterscotch-Peanut Banana, 163
    Chocolate, 162
    Choco-Pineapple Frosties, 150
    Deluxe Chocolate, 162
    Deluxe Strawberry, 163
    Frozen Banana Kabobs, 163
    Quik Covered, 162

Pots de Crème, 111

PUDDINGS

    Butterscotch Apple Crisp, 110
    Chocolate Charlotte Russe, 106
    Chocolate Cream Cups, 110
    Chocolate Heavenly Crown, 122
    Chocolate Puddin' Cake, 111
    Chocolate Velvet, 106
    Instant Pudding Parfait, 109
    "Laced" Chocolate Bavarian, 107
    Minted Float, 111
    Mocha Bavarian, 121
    Parfait Parisienne, 109
    Peach Crisp, 108
    Pots de Crème, 111
    Revel Pudding, 109
    Sweet Kabob Boat, 107
    see also Doughnut Desserts, Soufflés

Puffs, Crinkly (cookies), 84
Pumpkin Pie, Café, 101

PUNCH

    Golden Wedding, 178
    Hot Tea, 178
    Pink Elephant, 182
    Pink Party, 182
    Tokay Cordial, 179

Quick Party Bars, 49
Quik, Chocolate, 184
Quik Chocolate Frosting, 23
Quik Covered Pops, 162
Quik, Creamy, 184
Quik Egg Nog, Individual, 183
Quik Fudgies (candy), 136
Quik, Hot Cinnamon, 184
Quik Milky Fizzer, 184
Quik Nog, Creamy, 183
Quik Nog, Hot, 183
Quik 'n' Peanut, 183
Quik, Strawberry, 184
Quik Sundae Sauce, Hurry-Up, 166

Raspberry Shrub, 179
Ribbon Candies, 143
Revel Puddings, 109

Sand Tarts, 63
Sandies (cookies), 63
Sandwich Cookies, Crunchy, 85
Sandwich Crunch Bars, 47

SAUCES AND TOPPINGS

Butterscotch Sauce, 132
Candied Fruit Topping, 129
Chocolate Dips, 132
Chocolate Marshmallow Sauce, 131
Chocolate-Peanut Sauce, 129
Chocolate Quik Sauce, 133
Coffee Hard Sauce, 131
Creamy Chocolate Sauce, 130
Dark Magic Sauce, 131
Honey Peanut Butter Topping, 129
Hot Fudge Sauce, 131
Olympia Chocolate Sauce, 130
One, Two, Three Sauce, 128
Orange Marmalade Topping, 129
Pancake Nescafé Sauce, 133
Pineapple-Butterscotch Sauce, 129
Sour Cream Topping, 133
Speedy Fudge Sauce, 130
Strawberry Sauce, 132
Strawberry Whipped Cream
    Topping, 132

SAUCES, SUNDAE

Butterscotch Sundae, 167
Cocoa-Mallow, 166
Coffee, 167
EverReady, 167
Fudge, 167
Hurry-Up Quik, 166
Skillet, 166
Speedy Coffee, 166
Thin Chocolate, 166
see also Sauces and Toppings
Scandinavian Snappers (cookies), 65
Scotch Crispies (candy), 138
Scotch-Oat Prizes (cookies), 82
Scrabble Squares (candy), 141
Sherbet 'n' Tea Cooler, 180
Sherried Tea Flip, 179
Skillet Sundae Sauce, 166

SODAS

Brown Cow, 164
Choco-Berry Fizz, 165
Chocolate Quik Soda, 164
Nescafé Soda, 164
Strawberry Quik Soda, 164

SOUFFLES

Bain Marie Chocolat, 125
Brown Orchid, 125
Delicate Chocolate Cups, 122
Soufflé au Chocolat Froid, 126
Sour Cream Topping, 133

Sour Cream Velvet Frosting, 25
Stackmores (dessert), 109
Strawberry Butter Frosting, 26
Strawberry Cookies, 87
Strawberry Crispies (candy), 140
Strawberry Dessert Pancakes, 128
Strawberry Dessert Roll, 105
Strawberry Double-Frosted, 165
Strawberry Flip, 182
Strawberry Frosting, Fluffy, 26
Strawberry Fruit Balls, 144
Strawberry Kisses, 83
Strawberry Mousse, Frozen, 152
Strawberry-Pineapple Parfait, 163
Strawberry Pops, Deluxe, 163
Strawberry Quik, 184
Strawberry Quik Soda, 164
Strawberry Sauce, 132
Strawberry Sparkler, 181
Strawberry Tea, 178
Strawberry Whipped Cream, 132
Sugar Plum Trees, 145
Swedish Delicacies (cookies), 67
Sweet Kabob Boat, 107
Swiss Chews (cookies), 68
Swiss Chocolate Cake, 10
Swiss Fruit-Nut Cookies, 64
Syrian Coffee, 172

TEA

Hot Tea Punch, 178
Hot Tea Toddy, 177
Iced Tea Trims, 177
Nestea, 181
Piquant Mulled, 178
Strawberry, 178

Tea Garden Bracer, 180
Tea 'n' Sherbet Cooler, 180
Three-Tone Party Squares, 51
Toddy, Hot Tea, 177
Tokay Cordial, 179
Toll House Cookie Variations, 31-32
Toll House Marble Squares, 32
Toll House Marble Squares,
    "Easy-to-Make," 32
Toll House Original Cookies, 31
Torte, Mocha Nut, 123
Torte, New Orleans, 124
Triple Treat Pie, 102
Two-Tone Doughnut Crumble, 127
Two-Tone Mallow Bites, 146

WAFFLES

Waffles, Chocolate Dessert, 127
Walnut Chocolettes (candy), 141
West Indian Juleps, 171

*Nescafé, Nestea, Nestlé, Nestlé's Quik, EverReady and Toll House
are registered trademarks of The Nestlé Company, Inc.*